Mapbox Cookbook

Over 35 recipes to design and implement uniquely
styled maps using the Mapbox platform

Bill Kastanakis

[PACKT]
PUBLISHING

open source*
community experience distilled

BIRMINGHAM - MUMBAI

Mapbox Cookbook

First published: March 2016

Production reference: 1150316

Published by Packt Publishing Ltd.
Livery Place
35 Livery Street
Birmingham B3 2PB, UK.

ISBN 978-1-78439-735-7

www.packtpub.com

Credits

Author
Bill Kastanakis

Reviewer
Balkan Uraz

Commissioning Editor
Usha Iyer

Acquisition Editors
Vinay Argekar

Shaon Basu

Content Development Editor
Siddhesh Salvi

Technical Editors
Siddhesh Ghadi

Taabish Khan

Copy Editors
Shruti Iyer

Sonia Mathur

Project Coordinator
Nidhi Joshi

Proofreader
Safis Editing

Indexer
Mariammal Chettiyar

Production Coordinator
Conidon Miranda

Cover Work
Conidon Miranda

About the Author

Bill Kastanakis has been a software engineer for over 15 years with experience in desktop, mobile, and web application development. His love for the Mapbox platform came from a project he worked on in 2010 to build a series of iOS tourist guide apps. With maps being simplistic in appearance and their customization options being nearly zero, he discovered the potential of a platform that allows the developer to totally customize the appearance of maps and the experience of using them.

Bill currently owns MindBomb, which specializes in mobile apps for the iOS platform, and he is a cofounder of nCoded+ Limited, which builds enterprise mobile and web applications for casino accounting. He also works as an iOS team lead and architect for one of the most popular apps in Ireland.

Bill often contributes to presentations as well as writing several mobile development blogs about new mobile technologies.

About the Reviewer

Balkan Uraz is a city planner with a master's degree in Geographical Sciences. He has over 18 years of experience in the field of Geographic Information Systems.

Throughout his career, Balkan has worked on several projects with one thing in common: GIS. In the early days of his career, he worked on projects involving municipal GIS and city information systems. He has worked on major LBS projects for mobile operators in Turkey that involve both software development and building data inventories. He cofounded a tech company that specializes in navigation data collection and products. He has also been a GIS consultant for major companies operating in the areas of field tracking and real estate. In all his projects, he has worked around his one passion, which is building up spatial infrastructure.

Balkan is the coauthor of the book *Google Maps JavaScript API Cookbook* with Alper Dincer, published by Packt Publishing.

www.PacktPub.com

eBooks, discount offers, and more

Did you know that Packt offers eBook versions of every book published, with PDF and ePub files available? You can upgrade to the eBook version at www.PacktPub.com and as a print book customer, you are entitled to a discount on the eBook copy. Get in touch with us at customercare@packtpub.com for more details.

At www.PacktPub.com, you can also read a collection of free technical articles, sign up for a range of free newsletters and receive exclusive discounts and offers on Packt books and eBooks.

https://www2.packtpub.com/books/subscription/packtlib

Do you need instant solutions to your IT questions? PacktLib is Packt's online digital book library. Here, you can search, access, and read Packt's entire library of books.

Why Subscribe?

- ▶ Fully searchable across every book published by Packt
- ▶ Copy and paste, print, and bookmark content
- ▶ On demand and accessible via a web browser

Table of Contents

Preface

Maps are an essential element in today's location-aware applications, but they lack variation and customization. The Mapbox platform offers the tools and APIs required to totally customize, populate, and publish a map.

In this book, starting with the basics of Mapbox Editor for your first map styling steps, we will take you all the way to building advanced web and mobile applications with completely customizable map styles. The book focuses on the CartoCSS styling language as well as Mapbox tools and its JavaScript API, which inherits from Leaflet and is one of the most established, robust, and easy-to-use libraries.

We will then introduce two core Mapbox tools: TileMill and Mapbox Studio. Using them, we will generate custom-styled map tiles and vector maps. We will then move on to how to publish your custom maps using PHP, Node.js, and third-party tools such as GeoServer.

The next step is to start using the Mapbox JavaScript API and Leaflet to create different visualization map styles, such as a choropleth map and a heat map, and add user interactivity using UTFGrid.

We will continue with the advanced chapters and focus on integrating with third-party services such as Foursquare, Google Fusion Tables, CartoDB, and Torque to help us populate and even animate our maps.

Finally, we will end the book with a chapter dedicated to mobile devices. You will learn about Mapbox GL and how to create a fully functional, location-aware mobile app, which will use the map styles created in the earlier recipes.

This book is fast-paced, and the recipes are easy to follow. While it focuses on a recipe approach, it dives into the core concepts and theory of the technologies used to help you understand the theory required for GIS, web, and mobile development.

What this book covers

Chapter 1, Introduction to Mapbox, shows how to style your own base map using Mapbox Editor, add vector data, and publish your maps.

Chapter 2, Mapbox Services, shows how to use the lower-level Mapbox Web Services API to access data from the Mapbox servers.

Chapter 3, TileMill and Mapbox Studio, shows how to create stunning custom raster and vector maps using TileMill and Mapbox Studio.

Chapter 4, Mapbox.js, is an introduction to the Mapbox JavaScript API. This chapter will show how to create custom layers, add vector and raster data, and create interactivity and custom map styles such as choropleth and heat maps.

Chapter 5, Mapbox.js Advanced, shows how to use external data sources and integrate them with datasets from third-party services.

Chapter 6, Mapbox GL, shows how to create a fully functional mobile app using Mapbox GL for iOS.

What you need for this book

You require the following software:

- ▶ A code editor, such as Sublime Text, Atom or Brackets
- ▶ The latest versions of TileMill and Mapbox Studio
- ▶ The latest version of Xcode and a Mac computer
- ▶ GIS software, such as QGIS (this is optional)
- ▶ A REST client, such as Postman for Chrome or PAW for Mac (this is optional)

Who this book is for

Whether you are a web developer looking to dive into the GIS world or a GIS professional looking to create advanced web and mobile applications, this book is for you.

Sections

In this book, you will find several headings that appear frequently (Getting ready, How to do it, How it works, There's more, and See also).

To give clear instructions on how to complete a recipe, we use these sections as follows:

Getting ready

This section tells you what to expect in the recipe, and describes how to set up any software or any preliminary settings required for the recipe.

How to do it...

This section contains the steps required to follow the recipe.

How it works...

This section usually consists of a detailed explanation of what happened in the previous section.

There's more...

This section consists of additional information about the recipe in order to make the reader more knowledgeable about the recipe.

See also

This section provides helpful links to other useful information for the recipe.

Conventions

In this book, you will find a number of text styles that distinguish between different kinds of information. Here are some examples of these styles and an explanation of their meaning.

Code words in text, database table names, folder names, filenames, file extensions, pathnames, dummy URLs, user input, and Twitter handles are shown as follows: "We can include other contexts through the use of the `include` directive."

A block of code is set as follows:

```
#layer {
line-color: #C00;
line-width: 1;
}
```

When we wish to draw your attention to a particular part of a code block, the relevant lines or items are set in bold:

```
<iframe width='100%' height='500px' frameBorder='0'
src='https://a.tiles.mapbox.com/v4/nimrod7.k4adg5mg/attribution,zo
ompan,zoomwheel,geocoder,share.html?access_token=pk.eyJ1Ijoibmltcm
9kNyIsImEiOiJkNkw1WWRnIn0.pnQn9P2nbHyhKf2FY_XJog'></iframe>
```

Any command-line input or output is written as follows:

```
git clone https://github.com/mapbox/tilestream.git .
```

New terms and **important words** are shown in bold. Words that you see on the screen, for example, in menus or dialog boxes, appear in the text like this: "Copy the clipboard copy icon next to the **Share** textbox."

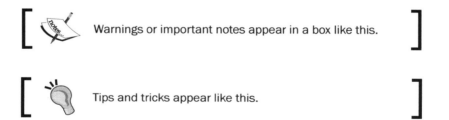

> Warnings or important notes appear in a box like this.

> Tips and tricks appear like this.

Reader feedback

Feedback from our readers is always welcome. Let us know what you think about this book— what you liked or disliked. Reader feedback is important for us as it helps us develop titles that you will really get the most out of.

To send us general feedback, simply e-mail feedback@packtpub.com, and mention the book's title in the subject of your message.

If there is a topic that you have expertise in and you are interested in either writing or contributing to a book, see our author guide at www.packtpub.com/authors.

Customer support

Now that you are the proud owner of a Packt book, we have a number of things to help you to get the most from your purchase.

Downloading the example code

You can download the example code files for this book from your account at `http://www.packtpub.com`. If you purchased this book elsewhere, you can visit `http://www.packtpub.com/support` and register to have the files e-mailed directly to you.

You can download the code files by following these steps:

1. Log in or register to our website using your e-mail address and password.
2. Hover the mouse pointer on the **SUPPORT** tab at the top.
3. Click on **Code Downloads & Errata**.
4. Enter the name of the book in the **Search** box.
5. Select the book for which you're looking to download the code files.
6. Choose from the drop-down menu where you purchased this book from.
7. Click on **Code Download**.

Once the file is downloaded, please make sure that you unzip or extract the folder using the latest version of:

- WinRAR / 7-Zip for Windows
- Zipeg / iZip / UnRarX for Mac
- 7-Zip / PeaZip for Linux

Downloading the color images of this book

We also provide you with a PDF file that has color images of the screenshots/diagrams used in this book. The color images will help you better understand the changes in the output. You can download this file from `https://www.packtpub.com/sites/default/files/downloads/MapboxCookbook_ColorImages.pdf`.

Errata

Although we have taken every care to ensure the accuracy of our content, mistakes do happen. If you find a mistake in one of our books—maybe a mistake in the text or the code—we would be grateful if you could report this to us. By doing so, you can save other readers from frustration and help us improve subsequent versions of this book. If you find any errata, please report them by visiting http://www.packtpub.com/submit-errata, selecting your book, clicking on the **Errata Submission Form** link, and entering the details of your errata. Once your errata are verified, your submission will be accepted and the errata will be uploaded to our website or added to any list of existing errata under the Errata section of that title.

To view the previously submitted errata, go to https://www.packtpub.com/books/content/support and enter the name of the book in the search field. The required information will appear under the **Errata** section.

Piracy

Piracy of copyrighted material on the Internet is an ongoing problem across all media. At Packt, we take the protection of our copyright and licenses very seriously. If you come across any illegal copies of our works in any form on the Internet, please provide us with the location address or website name immediately so that we can pursue a remedy.

Please contact us at copyright@packtpub.com with a link to the suspected pirated material.

We appreciate your help in protecting our authors and our ability to bring you valuable content.

Questions

If you have a problem with any aspect of this book, you can contact us at questions@packtpub.com, and we will do our best to address the problem.

1

Introduction to Mapbox

In this chapter, we will cover the following recipes:

- ▶ Creating your own map
- ▶ Adding vector data
- ▶ Publishing your map

Introduction

Most websites we visit every day use maps in order to display information about locations or points of interest to the user. It is amazing how this technology has evolved over the past few decades.

In the early days, with the introduction of the Internet, maps were static images. Users were unable to interact with maps as they were limited to just displaying static information. Interactive maps were available only to mapping professionals, accessed via very expensive GIS software. Cartographers used this type of software to create or improve maps, usually for an agency or an organization. Again, if information about a location was to be made available to the public, there were only two options: static images or a printed version.

Improvements in Internet technologies opened up possibilities for interactive content. It was a natural transition for maps to become live, respond to search queries, and allow user interactions, such as panning and changing the zoom level.

Mobile devices were just beginning to evolve, and a new age of smartphones was about to begin. It was natural for maps to become even more important to consumers. Interactive maps are now in their pockets, and more importantly, they can tell a user's location and display a great variety of data.

In an age in which smartphones and tablets have become aware of location, information has become even more important to companies. Smartphones use this information to improve user experience in everything from general-purpose websites such as Google Maps, to more focused apps such as Foursquare and Facebook. Maps are now a crucial component in the digital world.

The popularity of mapping technologies is increasing over the years. A number of services have become available to developers, from free open source solutions to commercial services for web and mobile developers, and even services specialized for cartographers and visualization professionals.

Currently, developers have the option to choose from a variety of services that will work better for their specific tasks. The best part of all is that if some customers have increased traffic requirements, most of them are offered free plans.

Getting started with Mapbox

The issue with most of the solutions available is that they look extremely similar. By observing the most commonly used websites and services that implement a map, you can easily confirm that they completely lack personality.

Maps have the same colors and present the same features, such as roads, buildings, and labels. Currently, displaying road addresses on a specific website doesn't make sense. Customizing maps is a tedious task, and that is the main reason that it's avoided. What if the map provided by a web service does not work well with the color theme used in your website or app?

Mapbox is a service provider that allows users to select from a variety of customization options. This is one of the most popular features that set it apart from its competitors. The power to fully customize your map in every detail, including the color theme, features you want to present to the user, information displayed, and much more, is indispensable. Using the tools provided by Mapbox, you can upload and publish your own datasets and integrate them with Mapbox's own data.

Mapbox provides you with the tools to fully write in **CartoCSS**, the language behind Mapbox's cartographic customization, SDKs, and frameworks, to integrate their maps into your website with minimal effort, along with a lot more tools to assist you in your task and provide your users with a unique experience.

Data

Let's take a look at what Mapbox has to offer. We will begin with the three available datasets.

Mapbox Streets is the core technology behind Mapbox's street data. It's powered by Open Street Maps and has an extremely vibrant community of 1.5 million voluntary cartographers and users, who constantly refine and improve map data in real time.

For more information regarding the Mapbox and Open Street Maps partnership, visit `https://www.mapbox.com/guides/osm-and-mapbox/`.

For more information regarding Open Street Maps, visit `http://www.openstreetmap.org`.

Mapbox Terrain is composed of datasets fetched from 24 other datasets owned by 13 organizations. It enables you to access elevation data, hill shades, and topography lines, as shown in the following figure:

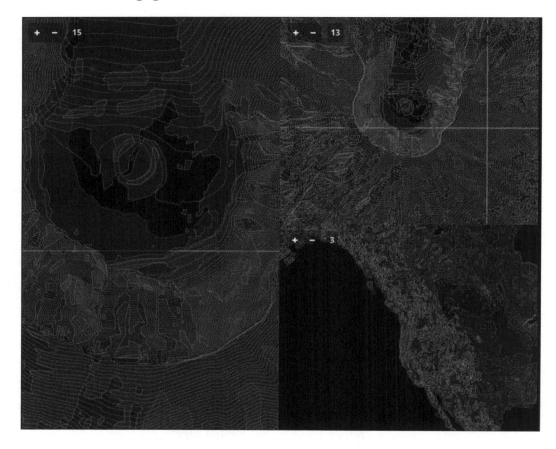

Mapbox Satellite offers high-resolution cloudless datasets with satellite imagery, as shown in the following figure:

Mapbox Editor

Mapbox Editor is an online editor with which you can easily create and customize maps. Its purpose is for you to easily customize the map's color theme by choosing from presets or creating your own styles. Additionally, you can add features such as markers and lines, or define areas using polygons. Maps are also multilingual, and currently there are four different languages as options to choose from while working with Mapbox Editor:

While adding data manually in Mapbox Editor is handy, it also offers the ability to *batch import data*, and it supports the most commonly used formats.

The user interface is *strictly visual*. No coding skills are needed in order to create, customize, and present a map. It is ideal if you want to quickly create and share maps. It also supports sharing to all major platforms, such as WordPress, and embedding in forums or websites using IFrames.

CartoCSS

CartoCSS is a powerful open source-style sheet language developed by Mapbox and widely supported by several other mapping and visualization platforms. It's extremely similar to CSS, and if you have ever used CSS, it will be very easy for you to adapt. Take a look at the following code:

```
#layer {
    line-color: #C00;
    line-width: 1;
}
#layer::glow {
    line-color: #0AF;
    line-opacity: 0.5;
    line-width: 4;
}
```

TileMill

TileMill is a free open source desktop editor that you can use to write CartoCSS and fully customize your maps. This is done by adding layers of data from various sources and then customizing layer properties using CartoCSS, a CSS-like style sheet language. When you complete the editing of the map, you can export the tiles and upload them to your Mapbox account in order to use the map on your website. TileMill was used as the standard solution for this type of work, but it used raster data. This changed with the introduction of Mapbox Studio, which uses vector data:

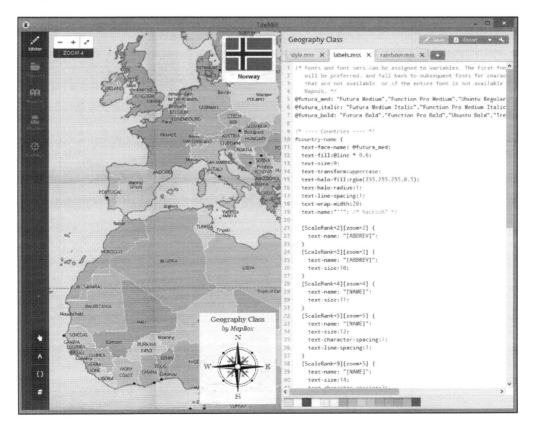

Mapbox Studio

Mapbox Studio is the new open source toolbox created by the Mapbox team to customize maps, and the plan is to slowly replace TileMill. The advantage is that it uses vector tiles instead of raster. Vector tiles are superior because they hold infinite detail; they are not dependent on the resolution found in a fixed-size image. You can still use CartoCSS to customize the map, and as with TileMill, you can export and share the map to your website at any point:

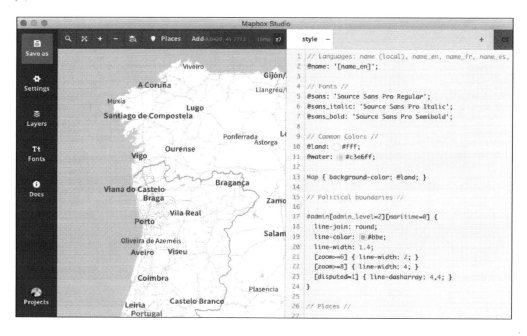

API and SDK

Accessing Mapbox data using various APIs is also very easy. You can use JavaScript or WebGL, or simply access the data using REST service calls. If you are into mobile development, separate SDKs are offered to develop native apps for iOS and Android that take advantage of the amazing Mapbox technologies and customization while maintaining a native look and feel.

Mapbox allows you to use your own sources. You can import a custom dataset and overlay the data on Mapbox Streets, Terrains, or satellite base maps. Another feature worth noting is that you are not limited to fetching data from various sources, as you can also query the tile metadata.

Creating your own map

In this recipe, you will be introduced to the core functionality of Mapbox Editor. In the beginning, we will explore the project management dashboard to create a new project. After this, we will use the interactive color picker provided by Mapbox Editor's user interface to help us style our new map.

The power of Mapbox Editor must not be underestimated. The functionality provided allows us to experiment with color schemes and gives our map a unique personality without writing a single line of code. The controls are simple, but at the same time there are options for sophisticated color mixing, making our task easier than ever.

Even if you advance deeper into the book and learn the secrets of CartoCSS, the powerful styling language that powers TillMill and Mapbox Studio, you will often use Mapbox Editor as a scratchpad to experiment with new ideas and color schemes.

Getting ready

To start working with Mapbox, you need to create a user account. This account is needed when you want to create a new project, use the editor, share data, and access the APIs for development; it is used to get a unique access token that you will use in the future when developing using the APIs.

Mapbox offers a free, non-time-limited plan that suffices for the scope of learning Mapbox as long as you do not have any heavy traffic on your published maps. There are limitations, especially when using Mapbox Studio, but you can start with a free plan and upgrade later when needed.

Head over to www.mapbox.com and click on **Sign up** in the upper-right corner. Follow the instructions to create a new account. After you have created it, simply sign in and select **Projects** from the menu:

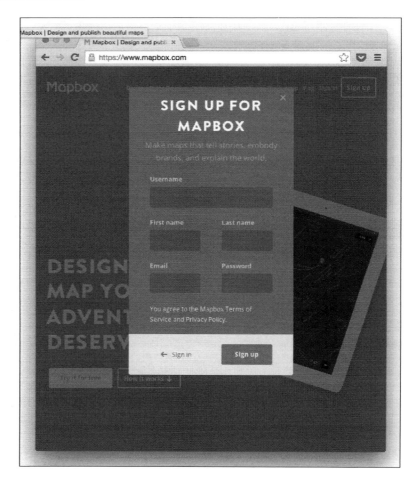

How to do it...

The first step is to create a new project:

1. Once you have signed in, you will be transferred to the **Projects** screen. From here, you can create new projects, edit them, or delete them. You will also see the default API access token at the top of the screen, but we will get to that a bit later:

2. Click on the **Create project** button, and you will be transferred to Mapbox Editor, where you can style or import data and save your map.

How it works...

You can pan simply by dragging the mouse on the map, and zoom using the mouse scroll wheel or the plus and minus buttons in the lower-left corner of the screen. Next to the zoom buttons, there is a handy box showing the current coordinates in latitude and longitude of the region currently on the screen. In the upper-left corner of the screen, you will see your profile picture and several buttons that give you access to the related sections. Next to the profile picture is **Style**, which is used to select one of the predefined map styles:

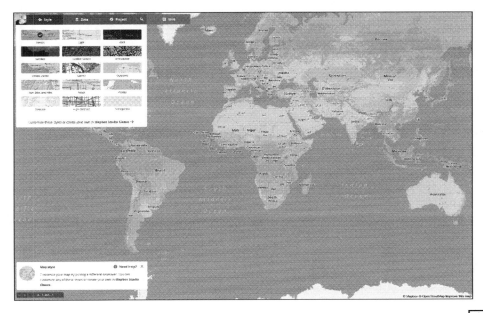

You can start customizing your map immediately by selecting one of the available preset styles to get started with a predefined color style. You can select any of the 15 available styles provided by Mapbox.

> There was a time when Mapbox allowed us to customize the color theme using Mapbox Editor.
>
> Sadly, this functionality has now been removed, and Mapbox kindly reminds us that we can use Mapbox Studio to customize our maps. Don't worry; in the end, it's much more powerful to do it this way, and we will learn more about it in *Chapter 3, TileMill and Mapbox Studio*.

Adding vector data

Getting ready

Most of the time, you will be presenting a map in order to guide the user to a specific location. You can add a variety of vector data to your map, which can be markers if you want to show a **POI (point of interest)** to the user; lines, which represent a route from one location to another; and polygons, which can be used if you want to highlight an entire area.

How to do it...

There are a number of things that we can do with vector data in Mapbox. Here are a few of them.

Creating a marker

The following steps need to be performed:

1. Click on **Data**.
2. Click on **Marker** and then click anywhere on the map. A marker will drop. You can adjust the marker's position by dragging it and dropping it at a different location.
3. Add any title you like on the marker.

4. For the description, you can use not only plain text, but also the `<img>` and `<a>` tags. Try adding the following code as the description:

```
Here is the location I told you about. Check out the
images. More information <a
href="http://www.wikipedia.com">here.</a> <img
src="http://lorempixel.com/400/200/city/"></img>
```

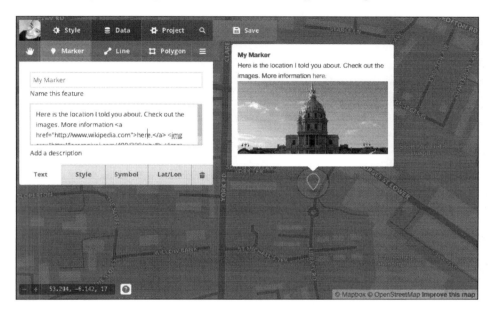

5. Click on the **Style** tab. You can select a color of your choice for the marker and also its size from three predefined sizes.

6. Click on the **Symbol** tab. Here, you can select an icon for your marker. Some personality is never bad!

7. The last tab is **Lat/Lon** (Latitude/Longitude). You can type in the exact coordinate if you feel so inclined.

Creating lines

Mapbox Editor gives you the ability to create lines. Routes, for example, are best represented with lines. Perform the following steps:

1. Click on the **Data** tab.

2. Click on **Line** and start the line by clicking anywhere on the map.

3. When you move the mouse, you will notice that Mapbox Editor shows you a dashed line; click on the next point of the map.

4. You can continue clicking and expanding your path as long as you wish. To complete the line, click on the last point again.

5. After you have completed the line, you can still modify each point by simply selecting a point and dragging it to a different location. If you click between two points, Mapbox Editor will create a new point.

6. Give your line a title and a description if you wish:

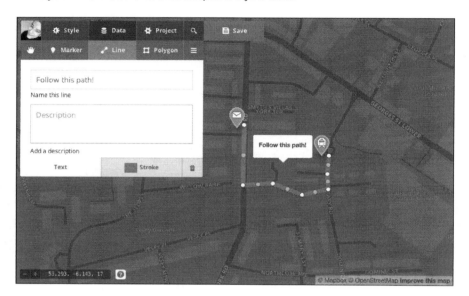

7. You can further customize the line style by selecting the **Stroke** option and choosing a color, a line width, and the opacity:

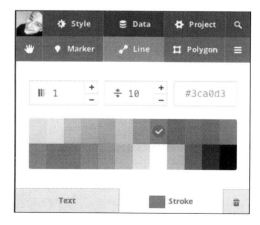

Creating polygons

There are times when you need to pinpoint a specific area to the user. While you can somehow archive this to an extent by enclosing the area using lines, there is a better and easier way, which is to use polygons:

1. Click on the **Data** tab.

2. Select **Polygon**.

3. Click anywhere in the map to start drawing the polygon.

4. Continue adding points on the map until you have the area of your choice selected. To complete the polygon, click on the first point again.

5. You can add a title and description if you wish.

6. At the **Stroke** tab, you can select a color, the line width, and the opacity of the outline, as with lines.

7. You can also select a fill color as well as the opacity of the filled color:

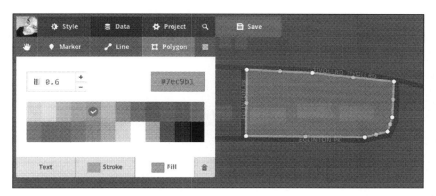

Modifying and deleting data

To modify a marker, line, or polygon, perform the following steps:

1. Simply select the hand tool and the item you want to adjust.

 Clicking on the button with three horizontal lines on the right-hand side of the **Polygon** tab (often called the **Hamburger** icon) displays a list of features. If you can't select something, you can use this menu to find the feature in question.

2. Mapbox Editor displays the properties of the selected objects and you can modify any of them, such as the title, description, or colors.

3. To delete a marker, line, or polygon, you have to select it with the hand tool and click on the small trash can icon in the lower-right corner.

There's more...

Importing data

We have seen how easy it is to add features such as markers, lines, and polygons. However, each time, we have to create them one by one.

This would be tedious if we wanted to create several hundred or even thousands of them. The import feature of Mapbox Editor does exactly this. It allows us to import several well-known file formats, such as GeoJSON, CVS, KML, and GPS. Most GIS software, organizations, and services out there are able to export in one of these formats; they are used widely in the GIS and web-development landscape all over the world.

It's probably a good time to explain what these formats are:

- **GeoJSON**: This is a format created to store vector data, such as points, lines, or polygons. It's based on the JSON specification.

- **KML**: This is used primarily by Google. It stores vector data as GeoJSON, but is based on XML.

- **GPX**: This is the format usually exported by GPS receivers.

- **CSV**: This is a format commonly used in popular applications, such as Excel. It's actually a comma-separated format, and in order to import a CVS file into Mapbox Editor, it requires at least a latitude and longitude column.

Each file can contain multiple layers. By layer, we mean multiple features that are grouped together.

We will import a GeoJSON file that contains earthquake data for the last seven days by performing the following steps:

1. Start a new project.

2. Click on **Discard Palette** to choose a preset style, or style your map from scratch if you prefer.

3. Ensure that the hand tool is selected. Directly below it, you will see **Draw or import .geojson, .cvs, .kml, or .gps files.** Click on **import**.

4. You will be greeted with the **Import features** dialog box. The provided GeoJSON file contains many different fields, such as the earthquake's magnitude, time, place, and so on. We can specify which of these fields will be displayed in the title and description. Ensure that **Title** is selected and select **mag** (magnitude) as the title field:

5. Next, select the **Description** tab and then select the **place** field as the description.

6. In the **Style** tab, select your preferred color and marker size.

7. In the **Symbol** tab, select any symbol you prefer.

8. Click on **Finish importing**:

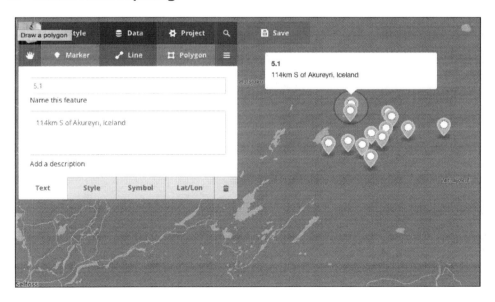

The map will zoom out, and the imported features will appear on the map with the fields that we selected as the title and description.

Editing imported data

You can access imported data by clicking on the hamburger icon on the data screen next to the polygon button. You will be presented with a list of every feature you imported. This section is composed of two tabs: the first one lists the features, and the other lists the layers. GeoJSON and KML are formats that can contain features grouped into multiple layers:

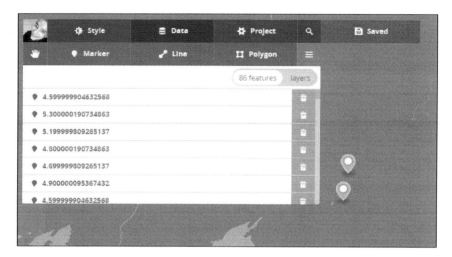

Clicking on an item in the featured list allows us to edit it. We can change the title, description, color, size, and icon of the feature where available, as different types of feature have different attributes that we can modify.

Clicking on the **trash can** icon next to an item allows us to delete these specific features.

Publishing your map

Now that we have created our own map and added the features we wanted, it's time to show it to the world.

In this recipe, we will learn how to publish our maps.

Getting ready

At this point, we have beautifully styled our map using Mapbox Editor and we have learned how to create data from scratch or import it. Now it's time for the world to see what we have created.

Before publishing your map, it's wise to have an overview of some settings that may be useful:

▶ Under **Project** | **Settings**, you can select the name of your project and its description

▶ Under **Project** | **Advanced**, you can set and save the current map position

Mapbox Editor offers various options for sharing our map. If you have created markers, lines, or polygons, or imported any data, you will be presented with an option to download them as GeoJSON or KML. You can use these files to overlay the data on a map using JavaScript or other APIs. We will take a look at how to do this in the next few chapters.

How to do it...

In order to share a Mapbox-hosted map, you will need to use the URL provided by Mapbox to directly share your map. Before doing this, however, in order to share it you need to first save the map:

1. Click on **Save**.

2. Copy the clipboard copy icon next to the **Share** textbox.

3. The URL will now be copied to the clipboard. Paste the link anywhere you want for the world to see:

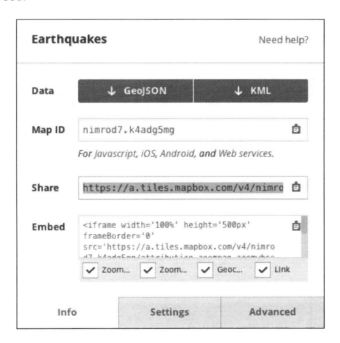

> The **Map ID** is used by Mapbox APIs to get access to this specific map. We will see how we can use it in the next few chapters.

Downloading the example code

You can download the code files by following these steps:

- Log in or register to our website using your e-mail address and password.
- Hover the mouse pointer on the **SUPPORT** tab at the top.
- Click on **Code Downloads & Errata**.
- Enter the name of the book in the **Search** box.
- Select the book for which you're looking to download the code files.
- Choose from the drop-down menu where you purchased this book from.
- Click on **Code Download**.

Once the file is downloaded, please make sure that you unzip or extract the folder using the latest version of:

- WinRAR / 7-Zip for Windows
- Zipeg / iZip / UnRarX for Mac
- 7-Zip / PeaZip for Linux

There's more...

Embedding a map in a self-hosted page

If you have a self-hosted website, the easiest option is to share your map using IFrames. You can also share to Wordpress, Tumblr, Drupal, and other platforms that support IFrames (usually via plugins).

Mapbox Editor already provides the code to embed the map into HTML.

Below the embedded textbox there are checkboxes. These allow us to limit user interaction in the embedded map. For example, you can disable **pan and zoom**, **scroll wheel....**, and **geocoding**, which disables the magnifier icon that allows us to search for addresses and links.

The code generated in the embed tag looks similar to this:

```
<iframe width='100%' height='500px' frameBorder='0'
src='https://a.tiles.mapbox.com/v4/nimrod7.k4adg5mg/attribution,zo
ompan,zoomwheel,geocoder,share.html?access_token=pk.eyJ1Ijoibmltcm
9kNyIsImEiOiJkNkw1WWRnIn0.pnQn9P2nbHyhKf2FY_XJog'></iframe>
```

Notice the `width` and `height` parameters. We can modify these to specify the size that will work best with our design. You can explicitly set the width or height to a specific pixel value or set a percentage.

Notice the `frameBorder` option. This generates a border around the IFrame to separate the embedded map from the content of the webpage.

For this example, we will use a basic HTML file that contains boilerplate HTML code and some extra elements. We will embed the map into HTML using IFrames.

From this point on, we will need to edit files and write code, usually HTML and JavaScript, and we will need an editor to do so. While a simple plain text editor, such as notepad on Windows and TextEdit on Mac, can do the job, it's highly recommended that you use a specialized application for this purpose, such as Sublime Text, which is available for Windows, Mac, and Linux. It can make our task a lot easier with syntax highlighting.

Before we begin editing HTML, double–click on the `chapter-1/example-1-begin/ index.html` file, and it will open in your default browser. You will see our HTML page, which contains some basic HTML elements such as `<h1>` and `<divs>` tags. Embed our map under the `<h3>Earthquakes in Iceland:</h3>` element through the following steps:

1. Open the `chapter-1/example-1-begin/index.html` file with a text editor.
2. Copy the code contained within the embedded tag.
3. Adjust the width and height if needed, and add a frame border if you wish.
4. Directly under `<h3>Our Location</h3>`, paste the code we copied before.
5. Save the file.

That's it. We have successfully embedded a map into a custom HTML page using the sharing feature of Mapbox Editor and IFrames. Now, it's time to discuss what we created. We need to open the file in a browser by either dragging the `index.html` file on a browser or double-clicking on it (this behavior may be overwritten by your HTML editor):

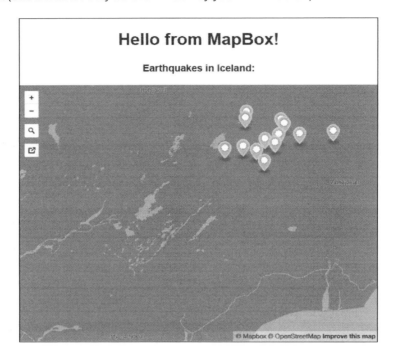

2
Mapbox Services

In this chapter, we will cover the following recipes:

- ▶ Accessing styled tiles on your map
- ▶ Creating static images
- ▶ Finding coordinates for an address
- ▶ Finding an address from coordinates
- ▶ Finding an address on a map click
- ▶ Getting directions

Introduction

Mapbox web services are the lowest-level API available on the platform. Every other API and functionality provided by Mapbox, such as the JavaScript API or Mapbox.js, is based on services. It uses GET REST calls to fetch the data you require from Mapbox servers.

REST services are based on HTTP verbs to perform certain actions, such as reading, creating, updating, and deleting records. **GET** requests are used to *read* data from the server; **PUT** requests are used usually to *update* data; **POST** requests are used to *create* a new record; and **DELETE** requests are used to *delete* a record. The Mapbox API is a read-only one, so we only have access to GET requests to read data.

Mapbox supports both HTTP and HTTPS secure connections. When the REST call is invalid, the server responds with the relative HTTP error code and a message in plain text, not a JSON object as usual.

Access tokens

To get access to the services, we will need an **access token**. We discussed access tokens in *Chapter 1, Introduction to Mapbox*, when we created a new project. This is a good moment to explain what an access token is.

Access tokens are *unique* to each account and our ticket to using Mapbox services and APIs. To be able to fetch data from Mapbox servers, the server has to identify us somehow, and providing our credentials is not a proper way to do this.

Using an access token, Mapbox knows which user is requesting data, which services are available to this user, and the bandwidth he/she uses. We are not supposed to share or publish access tokens. They should remain hidden at all costs; however, unfortunately, this is not always possible because in some cases—for example, when using JavaScript—the code, and therefore the access token, is included in the code and is easily accessible.

For this reason, Mapbox provides two different access tokens: the **public** access token and the **secret** access token. We use the public access token in places that will be exposed to the public; it is easy to access and replace. A secret access token is supposed to be used in places that remain secure and hidden, such as PHP code that will be evaluated on the server side or apps that will be compiled; changing it requires us to go through an approval process.

In the **Projects** dashboard, you may already have seen the public access token:

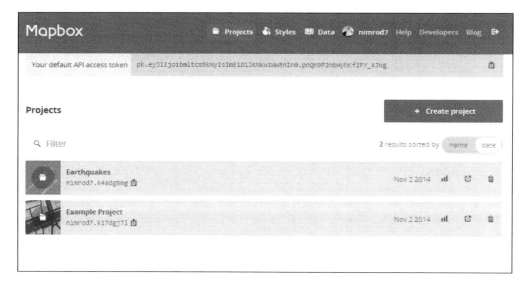

Clicking on the **API access token** link will open the **Apps** page, where you will find your secret access token:

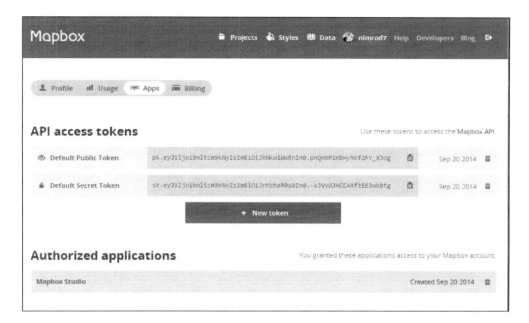

In this screen, you can find a list of applications that use the tokens.

You can also generate a new access token by clicking on the **New token** button in the middle of the screen. A window will open, allowing you to generate a public or secret access token, and in case of a secret token, you can define the scope.

Finding the Map ID

The second element that we need to use throughout this chapter is the **Map ID**. Each time we create a new map using Mapbox, it has a *unique* Map ID, and each time we perform a request, we have to pass the Map ID to tell Mapbox which map we are interested in.

You can find your Map ID in two different places:

▸ In the **Projects** dashboard, the Map ID is displayed directly below your map's name, and you can click on the clipboard icon next to it to copy it

> ▶ In Mapbox Editor, you can find it in the **Project** tab:

Accessing styled tiles on your map

We can use Mapbox services to fetch specific tiles from the service. To do so, we will use the GET HTTP verb to request the tile from Mapbox servers.

The advantage with REST GET requests is that you don't even need special tools or knowledge to call them.

I will present four methods that do not require coding, are easy to use, and will help us get through the chapter.

How to do it...

Here are the four ways:

> ▶ **Copy and paste the URL in your browser**: Yes, as simple as that! You can simply paste the URL in the web browser, and it will automatically perform the request for you. Although, it's not generally recommended to do it this way; I highly recommend that you use a specialized tool for this task from the ones mentioned in the following points.

▶ **Use a third-party online tool**: You can also use a third-party online tool, such as `https://www.hurl.it/`, to do REST calls.

▶ **Use a browser extension**: For Chrome, I suggest **PostMan**, which can be found at `https://chrome.google.com/webstore/detail/postman-rest-client/fdmmgilgnpjigdojojpjoooidkmcomcm?hl=en`:

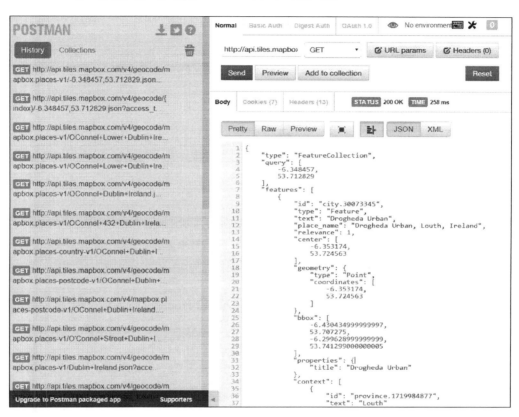

For Firefox, you may use the **RestClient** plugin, which can be found at `https://addons.mozilla.org/en-US/firefox/addon/restclient/`.

▶ **Use a native OS app**: For OS X, **Paw** by Lucky Marmot is an excellent choice, and you can get this at `https://luckymarmot.com/paw`:

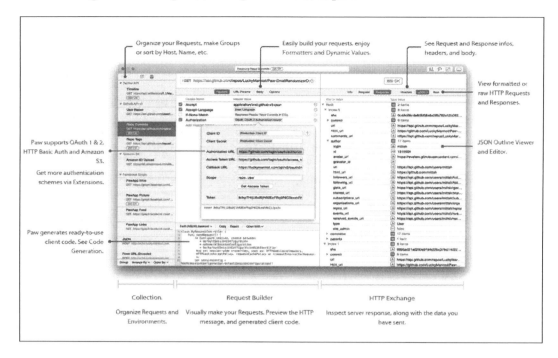

For a Windows system, you can try **Fiddler** from `http://www.telerik.com/download/fiddler`.

How it works...

Let's dissect the following URL to better understand what goes on by examining each parameter:

```
http://api.tiles.mapbox.com/v4/{mapid}/{z}/{x}/{y}.{format}?access_
token=<your access token>
```

▶ `http://api.tiles.mapbox.com`: All requests to Mapbox services must begin with `http://api` or `https://api`; then, we tell the services that we are interested in fetching individual `.tiles`.

- ▶ `v4`: This is the version number of the API. This ensures that your app doesn't break if the Mapbox team updates the API.

> Mapbox services is an API, and APIs often change or improve. Changing an API directly is not an option as it breaks every app out there that uses the changed function(s).
>
> The way it happens is usually by creating a new version of the API. Mapbox, at this moment, is at version 4, so apps that use a lower version don't need to be modified if they do not want to take advantage of the API functionality provided in the newer version. We will use the fourth version of their API for the examples in this book, which is the latest available at the moment.

- ▶ `{MapID}`: Replace this parameter with your Map ID. Each map has a unique Map ID that needs to be referenced here in order to access our styled tiles.

- ▶ `/z/x/y/`: These are integers with the coordinates of the specific tile. They are not latitude and longitude coordinates (which are two doubles, anyway), but these are coordinates based on the XYZ tiling scheme. The `z` parameter is the zoom level, while `x` and `y` are the tile numbers in the coordinate.

> A valid question at this point is how to get the *x* and *y* coordinates for the area you are interested in at a specific zoom level. There are numerous ways to convert latitude and longitude into the XYZ scheme.
>
> An excellent resource to get started is available at `http://wiki.openstreetmap.org/wiki/Slippy_map_tilenames`. It explains the mathematical equations behind the XYZ tiling scheme, provides code to a huge variety of programming languages, and even scripts in Python and Ruby that convert latitude and longitude to XYZ.
>
> An easy, hassle-free way is to use the online tool at `http://www.maptiler.org/google-maps-coordinates-tile-bounds-projection/`.

- ▶ `{format}`: You can choose the format of the tiles. Acceptable formats are PNG, from 16 colors to 256 colors, and JPG, with compression levels 60, 70, and 80n. The format can be prefixed with `@2x` for retina display.

By **retina display**, we mean the high resolution screens of mobile (and most recently desktop) devices, such as the iPhone. The retina term was introduced back in 2010 with the release of iPhone 4, in which the device display had a resolution of 640 x 960 pixels and a pixel density of 326 ppi (pixels per inch).

A screen this small in size and, at the same time, so dense in pixels, required special attention from developers. If an image with the original resolution is displayed on this screen as is, it will appear very small, and if it's scaled up at double size without doubling the number of pixels, it will appear jagged or blurry.

For optimal results, developers needed to supply the image in two different resolutions: the native (@1x) one and one that has twice the number of pixels or is double the size (@2x). The OS frameworks at runtime chose which resolution was appropriate for the specific display to ensure optimal quality. Retina screens are not limited to mobile devices; several laptops and screens from Apple and other manufacturers offer retina display.

Our tiles are simply images, and displaying these images in retina display would introduce the same issues.

▶ `access_token=<your access token>`: Finally, you need to supply your access token.

Now that you have understood how the GET request works, we can easily try it on a web browser. Build the URL by replacing the Map ID with the one of the map you plan to display and the access token with your own.

There's more...

Fetching a single tile

Fetching a single tile requires the following steps to be performed:

1. Find the tile you are interested in fetching.

2. Construct the HTTP GET request by providing the Map ID, tile, format, and access token; for example, consider the following URL:

   ```
   http://api.tiles.mapbox.com/v4/nimrod7.k4adg5mg/6/31/20.
   png?access_token=pk.eyJ1Ijoibmltcm9kNyIsImEiOiJkNkw1WWRnIn0.
   pnQn9P2nbHyhKf2FY_XJog
   ```

3. Paste this URL in the browser or in a REST client.

Creating static images

Using Mapbox services, you can easily create static images in your map. Static images are useful because you may want to limit the user from exploring other areas. Plus, if this is the case, it will save bandwidth from your hosted Mapbox account.

How to do it...

Let's dissect the following Mapbox services request. Most of the request remains the same as the individual tiles' requests in the previous recipe. One important difference is that this time, we provide the latitude, longitude, and zoom level instead of individual tile numbers, as follows:

```
http://api.tiles.mapbox.com/v4/nimrod7.k4adg5mg/{lon},{lat},{z}/
{width}x{height}.{format}?access_token=<your access token>
```

- ▶ {lon}: This is the longitude; coordinates range from -180 to 180 using a decimal separator.
- ▶ {lat}: This is the latitude; coordinates range from -85 to 85 using a decimal separator.
- ▶ {z}: This is the zoom level supported by them and integer ranging from 1 to 19.
- ▶ {width}: This is the image width in pixels. There are maximum 1280 pixels.
- ▶ {height}: This is the image's height in pixels. There are maximum 1280 pixels.

Creating the static map

To do this, perform the following steps:

1. Find the latitude and longitude. One way is to use the Mapbox Editor to navigate to the location you are interested in. The latitude and longitude are displayed at the bottom of the map.

   Another way is to use an online service, such as http://itouchmap.com/latlong.html. This gives you the latitude and longitude for a specific point.

2. Construct the HTTP GET request by providing the Map ID, tile, format, and access token.

3. Paste the URL in the browser or in a REST client:

Adding a marker

Mapbox offers the ability to add markers to your static maps. The format of the requests has to be similar to the following:

```
{size}-{icon}+{color}({lon},{lat})
```

Here are the parameters you need to know:

> ▸ `{size}`: This is the size of the marker. The value accepted in this parameter is `pin-s` for small, `pin-m` for medium, and `pin-l` for large markers.

> ▸ `{icon}`: This is the marker icon. You can choose from a variety of icons offered by Mapbox services.

 Check out the Maki icons to get an idea of which icons you can use on your markers from `https://www.mapbox.com/maki/`.

> ▸ `{color}`: This is the color value in hex format. It can be three or six digits.

> ▸ `{lon}`: This is the longitude.

> ▸ `{lat}`: This is the latitude.

The following are the steps you need to perform:

1. Construct the HTTP GET request as in the previous recipe.
2. Add the marker after {MapID}.
3. Paste the URL in the browser or in a REST client.

The complete request should look similar to the following example:

```
http://api.tiles.mapbox.com/v4/nimrod7.k4adg5mg/pin-l-danger+f00(-
6.240,53.348)/-6.245079,53.344731,14/800x600.png?access_token=pk.
eyJ1Ijoibmltcm9kNyIsImEiOiJkNkw1WWRnIn0.pnQn9P2nbHyhKf2FY_XJog
```

Finding coordinates for an address

There are times when you have an address or just a city or a country, and you try to find the coordinates (latitude and longitude). The reverse is also true; you may have the latitude and longitude and want to get an address. This process is called **geocoding**.

Reverse geocoding is useful if, for example, we create a marker using the latitude and longitude and want to show the marker's address. Mapbox services also give you the ability to get the coordinates (latitude and longitude) from an address; this process is called **forward geocoding**.

How to do it...

The following steps need to be performed:

1. Construct a GET request by specifying the **master source** and **query**.
2. Paste the request in the browser or in a REST client.

   You will get back a JSON with coordinates that match your query.

The format of the requests has to be similar to the following:

```
{dataset}/{lon},{lat}.json?access_token=<your access token>
```

A complete request will look similar to the following example:

```
http://api.tiles.mapbox.com/v4/geocode/mapbox.
places-v1/OConnel+Dublin+Ireland.json?access_token=pk.
eyJ1Ijoibmltcm9kNyIsImEiOiJkNkw1WWRnIn0.pnQn9P2nbHyhKf2FY_XJog
```

If you try to execute the query as it is here, you will notice that the geocoder returns an array of results sorted by *relevance*, which is also the key name that has a float value. The result appearing at the top is the one that matches your query the most and has a higher value, while the others may have partial matches with your query:

How it works...

We will look at it from two perspectives.

Query parameters

The first question to ask yourself is, what do you need exactly from the Mapbox services geocoder? You may need just postcodes, or addresses, or the full stack, including every detail for the specified coordinates.

First of all, let's dissect a forward geocoding request:

```
http://api.tiles.mapbox.com/v4/geocode/{master-source}/{query}.
json?access_token=<your access token>
```

The parameter to choose what you want back from the geocoder is called a master source.

The available master sources are the following:

▶ `mapbox.places-v1`: This sends back every detail, including address, province, postcode, and so on.

▶ `mapbox.places-country-v1`: This sends back just the countries.

▶ `mapbox.places-province-v1`: This sends back the provinces.

▶ `mapbox.places-postcode-v1`: This sends back the postcodes. Postcodes are separated by country; for example, you can use `mapbox.places-postcode-fr-v1` to get back postcodes in France or `mapbox.places-postcode-uk-v1` to get back postcodes in the UK.

▶ `mapbox.places-city-v1`: This sends back places, such as cities.

▶ `mapbox.places-address-v1`: This sends back addresses.

The next parameter we need to know is the query itself. The query can be as detailed as you want; for example, you can just specify Ireland as a parameter, the city Dublin through `Dublin+Ireland`, O'Connel street through `OConnel+Dublin+Ireland`, or the street number 432 through `OConnel+432+Dublin+Ireland`.

Depending on the accuracy of the query, the geocoder may return a single result or multiple results as an array that matches the criteria you specified.

Returned results

You have probably noticed that this is the first time that we will get back data instead of images. There is an important parameter in each request that defines the kind of format Mapbox services will return to us.

The most common formats returned by REST services are **XML (Extensible Markup Language)** and **JSON (JavaScript Object Notation)**.

XML used to rule the world, but most services these days use JSON, which is faster to submit and easier to process and read. Mapbox services, at the moment, support only the JSON format.

Let's examine a partial JSON response from the geocoder, as follows:

```
{
            "id": "city.10560743",
            "type": "Feature",
            "text": "Dublin",
            "place_name": "Dublin, Dublin City, Ireland",
            "relevance": 0.48,
            "center": [
                -6.300364,
                53.333637
            ]
}
```

You will notice that there are curly brackets { } and square brackets [ ]. The latter represents an array of values, while the curly brackets represent an object. Each object may include other arrays, objects, or just key-values.

Key-values are represented with the key first, then with a double colon (:), and then with the value; here, the value may be a string, integer, float, or array. Using this specific format is very easy and efficient because *you can simply ask to get the value* using a key, which is the *same* in every request.

Using the preceding example, you can get the place name simply using this specific key, and the returned object will be "Dublin, Dublin City, Ireland" or the relevant value for other similar requests.

Finding an address from coordinates

The exact opposite of the process we saw just now is to provide the coordinates and get back an address, which is called reverse geocoding.

Let's examine the request structure, which is as follows:

```
http://api.tiles.mapbox.com/v4/geocode/{index}/{lon},{lat}.
json?access_token=<your access token>
```

At this point, it won't trouble you any more to find what is needed. Apart from index, this time, we need to provide the latitude and longitude.

How to do it...

Perform the following steps:

1. Construct a GET request by specifying the master source, latitude, and longitude.

2. Paste the request in the browser or in a REST client.

   You will get back a JSON file with coordinates matching your query.

A complete reverse geocoding query will look similar to this:

```
http://api.tiles.mapbox.com/v4/geocode/mapbox.
places-v1/-6.348457,53.712829.json?access_token=pk.
eyJ1Ijoibmltdcm9kNyIsImEiOiJkNkw1WWRnIn0.pnQn9P2nbHyhKf2FY_XJog
```

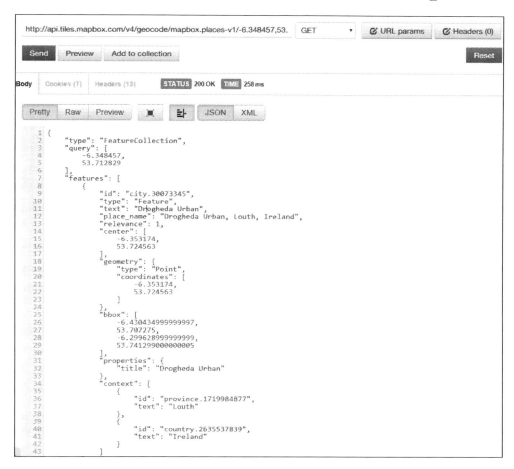

Finding an address on a map click

Now that we are learning to construct a GET request using Mapbox services, it's time to apply our knowledge in a real application.

We will use a simple JavaScript with Mapbox.js to make our lives easier. Don't worry about Mapbox.js; we have an entire chapter dedicated to it.

How to do it...

Perform the following steps for this:

1. Inside the `<script>` tag, begin by creating a variable for the access token, as follows:

```
var accessToken = 'pk.eyJ1Ijoibmltcm9kNyIsImEiOiJkNkw1WWRnInO.
pnQn9P2nbHyhKf2FY_XJog';
```

2. Then, pass the access token to Mapbox using the following code:

```
L.mapbox.accessToken = accessToken;
```

3. Now, get the element that holds the address box using the following code:

```
var click = document.getElementById('click');
```

4. Next, create a Mapbox `map` object and pass the initial coordinates and the zoom level by executing the following code:

```
var map = L.mapbox.map('map', 'nimrod7.k4adg5mg').
setView([51.492842, -0.131874], 16);
```

5. Create a `click` event on your map so that each time a user clicks on it, the included code is triggered:

```
map.on('click', function(e) {

  // Insert code in here

});
```

6. Inside the `click` handler, get the longitude and latitude, and create a string separated by a comma:

```
var latlong = e.latlng.lng + ',' + e.latlng.lat;
```

7. Construct a `url` variable using the base URL from the GET request, followed by the `latlong` variable and `accessToken`:

```
var url = 'http://api.tiles.mapbox.com/v4/geocode/mapbox.
places-v1/'+ latlong +'.json?access_token=' + accessToken;
```

8. Create a new `xmlHttp` request object. You can use it to submit the GET request, as follows:

```
xmlHttp = null;
xmlHttp = new XMLHttpRequest();
xmlHttp.open("GET", url, false);
xmlHttp.send();
```

9. Get the response back from the service. It will be a string, so convert it to a JSON object as follows:

```
var responseJSON = JSON.parse(xmlHttp.responseText);
```

10. Get the elements that are under the `'features'` key, then the first object `[0]`, and finally the element under the `'place_name'` key, as shown in the following line:

```
var placename = responseJSON['features'][0]['place_name'];
```

11. Pass `placename` to the `innerHTML` element with the following script:

```
window[e.type].innerHTML = placename;
```

That's it!

Open the HTML file in your browser and click on a location to get the address:

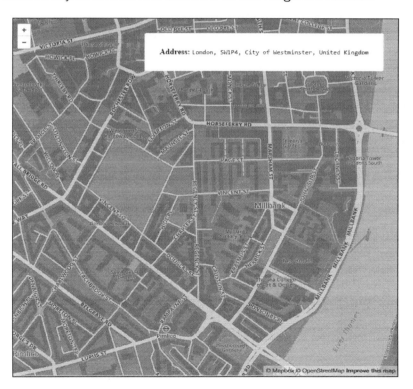

How it works...

In the example application, we will use Mapbox to display our map. When the user clicks on a map, we will submit a GET request to the Mapbox geocoder. The GET request will include the coordinates of the location that the user clicked on in the map.

Open `chapter-2/example-2-begin/index.html` in the HTML editor of your choice. The example includes a basic HTML5 boilerplate code.

At `<head>`, we will link Mapbox.js and stylesheet using the following lines of code:

```
<script src='https://api.tiles.mapbox.com/mapbox.js/v2.1.4/mapbox.js'>
</script>
<link href='https://api.tiles.mapbox.com/mapbox.js/v2.1.4/mapbox.css'
rel='stylesheet' />
```

Then, at the `<style>` tag, we will do some basic styling for the map and the box that displays the address.

We will use two `<div>` elements: one of them, with `id='output'`, will hold the address box, and the other, with `id='map'`, will include our map.

Getting directions

The Directions API is still in development by Mapbox and currently experimental. It will most likely evolve in the near future. For the moment, it supports only the driving directions.

 At the moment of writing this chapter, the Mapbox Directions API is available only when using a paid Mapbox plan.

How to do it...

You will need to perform the following steps:

1. Construct a GET request by specifying the profile and locations.

2. Paste the request in the browser or in a REST client.

   You will get back a JSON file with coordinates matching your query.

A complete request should look similar to the following one:

```
https://api.mapbox.com/v4/directions/mapbox.
driving/-6.260319,53.349786;-6.267706,53.340820.json?access_token=pk.
eyJ1IjoibWFwYm94cmVjaXBlcyIsImEiOiJjd3RhQmlzIn0.Wx0fWGCo3gs6fzta5QrLfw
```

How it works...

Let's dissect the following request:

```
http://api.tiles.mapbox.com/v4/directions/{profile}/{waypoints}.
json?access_token=<your access token>
```

> ▸ `{profile}`: This currently supports `mapbox.driving`, `mapbox.walking`, or `mapbox.cycling` as parameters:
>
>   ❑ `mapbox.driving`: This is great for motorcycle or car routing. This option is used by people who prefer taking highways for higher speed.
>
>   ❑ `mapbox.walking`: This is ideal for pedestrian or hiking routing. It shows the shortest path using sidewalks and trails.
>
>   ❑ `mapbox.cycling`: This is useful for bicycle routing. This option is used by someone who avoids highways and prefers streets with bike lanes.

> ▸ `{waypoints}`: Here, we will define a comma-separated list of locations. Each location must have a longitude and latitude parameter. The minimum number of waypoints is two: an origin and a destination. You can include more locations up to the limit of 25 if you are planning a long trip!
>
>   The waypoint format should be longitude and latitude separated by a semicolon, as follows: *-6.260319, 53.349786;-6.2403, 53.340820*

There are also a number of query parameters that you can define, which are as follows:

> ▸ `alternatives`: This parameter is a Boolean one, and if it is set to `true`, it allows the service to generate alternate routes.

> ▸ `instructions`: This parameter sets the format of the instructions returned by the service. It can be text or HTML.

> ▸ `geometry`: This parameter can be `GeoJSON`, `polyline`, or `false`.

Query parameters are attached after the question mark character (?) in the request, and each parameter must be separated from the other with the ampersand (&) character. For example, if you want to use `alternatives` and `instructions`, you need to attach `&alternatives=true&instructions=html` at the end of the request, as follows:

```
?access_token=pk.
eyJ1Ijoibmltltcm9kNyIsImEiOiJkNkw1WWRnIn0.
pnQn9P2nbHyhKf2FY_XJog&alternatives=true&instructions=h
tml
```

Have a look at the following screenshot:

In the preceding request, we performed a query to get driving directions from O'Connell Street to Golden Lane in Dublin. We used Postman to perform the request and the server response with the directions as a JSON object.

The most important keys in the response are the following:

- ▶ `origin`: This represents the starting point of the route. It may also contain a name.
- ▶ `destination`: This represents the end point of the route.
- ▶ `waypoints`: This is an array of objects representing the intermediate waypoints.
- ▶ `routes`: This is an array of alternative routes. They are ordered by descending recommendation ranks. They contain the following properties:
    - ❑ `distance`: This represents the distance in meters.
    - ❑ `duration`: This estimates the travel duration in seconds.
    - ❑ `summary`: This is a short summary of the route.
    - ❑ `geometry`: This represents the geometry of the route in a GeoJSON LineString or Polyline format (depending on which `geometry` parameter is set on the request).
    - ❑ `steps`: This is an array of route steps. A step is the smallest unit in a route; for example, it could be a turn. The `maneuver` object in `steps` defines what type of step it is. The `steps` object also contains the travel distance to the subsequent step, the duration, the cardinal direction, and the heading.

3
TileMill and Mapbox Studio

In this chapter, we will cover the following recipes:

- ▶ Styling a map with TileMill
- ▶ Styling a map with Mapbox Studio
- ▶ Publishing your base map on your server with PHP
- ▶ Publishing your base map on your server with Node.js

Introduction

Up until now, we have used Mapbox Editor to create and customize our maps. We have seen how feature-rich and powerful it is and how, using just a web interface to customize your map, it provides you with so many possibilities. We were able to totally customize the color theme, add markers and features, and customize their appearance.

Although powerful, there are times when *you need more control*. What if we want to change the widths of the lines that represent roads? What if we want to totally customize this width over different zoom levels? What if we want a custom font, or even better, a different font (or font size) at each zoom level? What if we want to hide or show features when a user zooms in or out?

The possibilities are endless, and the power of unlocking this level of customization lies in a language called **CartoCSS**. Well, it's not exactly a language like C++ or PHP, with objects and complicated memory management, but it is a much more user-friendly, stylesheet-like language that shares a lot of similarities with the well-known CSS.

Let's look at an overview of what we have just learned. We know that CartoCSS is an easy-to-use language that allows us to fully customize our maps. Does this sound too good to be true? There's more!

There are a lot of ways to write CartoCSS, and Mapbox provides us with two awesome tools that help us create, edit, and share our maps.

The first one is called **TileMill**, which is a well-known solution that has been offered for a number of years now. The other candidate is the new and shiny **Mapbox Studio**.

Let's begin by explaining what TileMill is and what it is useful for.

Understanding TileMill

TileMill is a standalone application that helps us add various layers of (map or vector) data, write CartoCSS, preview the results, and finally export the tiles:

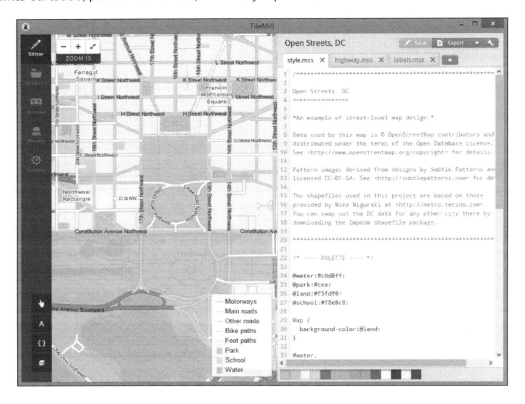

To better understand how it works, we will explain the workflow to create, customize, and publish our own custom-styled map.

If you open TileMill and create a new project, you will notice that it only shows a global map with coastlines. If you try to zoom in, you will see that there are no roads, labels, or other details—just a solid white color for land and blue for water. In order to start working with TileMill, you need to import the data you need.

TileMill supports a variety of data from different sources; for example, it allows us to import **shapefiles**, which contain geographical points, lines, or polygons. Using shapefiles, you can import features such as roads, coastlines, and buildings. Shapefiles support a single geometry type.

It also supports **GeoJSON**, a flexible file format that supports different geometry types. Many agencies provide data in this format; for example, if you request data for earthquakes in the last *n* days, you will receive a GeoJSON file that includes points indicating the recent earthquake locations.

You can even create images, such as **GeoTIFF** files, with data that you may want to overlay on your maps. This feature is extremely flexible; for example, you may want to overlay weather data, such as clouds, on top of your maps.

KML is another supported format popularized by Google. However, TileMill does not support many of the features of KML, such as images, flythroughs, and embedded styles, so keep this in mind when importing KML files.

TileMill also supports importing data from databases such as SQLite and PostGIS, which is an extension of PostgreSQL. You can connect directly from TileMill to a database and run queries.

Each separate file must be imported in a separate context, which TileMill calls a layer. Each layer can then be separately styled using CartoCSS. We can use the attributes found in the layer and style them differently. Once we have imported and styled all the layers, the last step is to export the map in order to publish it. We cannot simply export a huge image from it because, even for tiny areas with a zoom level of 15 or similar, it would export an immersive image in a size that would *not be possible for a normal computer to read due to memory limitations.*

For this reason, TileMill splits this huge image into separate tiny tiles. These tiles are then uploaded to Mapbox and displayed to the user.

 If you have ever noticed a map loading on a slow connection, you must have seen tiles appearing as the map loads.

Well, at this point, I imagine that you have begun to understand how powerful the whole process must be to import any data we want in different formats, combine them all together using layers, and style them individually with absolute control!

Now that you understand how TileMill works and how awesome it is, it's time for us to discuss the bad side of it. First of all, there is no easy way to import data that you want in it. You cannot just say, "let's zoom to San Francisco and style the map". You will have to import San Francisco into TileMill with all the features required, such as roads, water, labels, and buildings. Well, TileMill understands specific formats, so finding the exact data needed or extracting it from a source, such as **OpenStreetMap**, in a format that TileMill understands may be a tedious task. Luckily for us, there are websites that do exactly this, at least for major cities, so you may find everything you need on a website.

The second major drawback of TileMill is exporting the tiles. Exporting tiles even for small areas at a reasonable zoom level may require *thousands of images to be generated*. These images take time to be exported, consume large amounts of hard drive space, require huge storage on the server that we plan to host them on (for example, Mapbox), and also require a lot of time to upload hundreds of megabytes of tiles to this web server, especially if we have a low upload speed. *The overall process may take from minutes to hours and even days*, depending on the area's size and zoom level.

Luckily, we are talking about TileMill, which the Mapbox folks consider to be "old technology". For this reason, they developed Mapbox Studio.

Let's now see what Mapbox Studio is all about and how it compares with TileMill.

Understanding Mapbox Studio

Mapbox Studio was released a while ago to the public, and it is supposed to replace TileMill over time. Mapbox Studio uses vector data to represent maps, and, unlike TileMill, it's not based on bitmap tiles:

Let's find out how Mapbox Studio works.

We learned in the previous section that we need to import our data into TileMill. Well, this is not the case with Mapbox Studio because we immediately have access to Mapbox Streets, Mapbox Terrain, and Mapbox Satellite data. We do not need to search for the region of interest, extract it, and use it, as we do in the case of TileMill. With this simple choice, we can have access to data from the entire world down to the *finest* detail.

We can use Mapbox Streets as a source; this provides us with the vector data required to build a map. We can also select one of the other sources of Mapbox, such as Mapbox Terrain or Mapbox Satellite. We can even combine all these sources and overlay them one on top of the other to use the features provided by these different sources.

You may ask, what if I want to import and use my custom data and then overlay it on top of these maps? Well, this is easy too. You can import your own data into Mapbox Studio by converting data from traditional formats, such as those supported by TileMill. Once it is imported, you can then upload it to your Mapbox account, and it will immediately become available for use as a source in Mapbox Studio. It can then be overlaid on top of other map data.

Mapbox Studio works with vector tiles, and because of this, we do not need to export the resulting styled map in separate tiles. With Mapbox Studio, we will simply upload our own custom-created map into our Mapbox account—just like that! We don't have the hassle of waiting for hours for the tiles to be exported, neither do we need tons of hard drive space, and we are not required to have a high upload speed in order for the upload to be completed in reasonable time. The whole process is nearly *instantaneous*.

In spite of the importing and exporting capabilities of Mapbox Studio and the differences from TileMill in the technologies that it uses, such as the vector tiles, we still find a CartoCSS editor, and we can style our map using CartoCSS just as with TileMill.

Another handy feature of Mapbox Studio is the ability to automatically adapt to high-resolution displays (retina displays). In the case of TileMill, we need to export a separate double-sized tileset to use with these displays, causing the exported time, hard drive space, and upload time to double.

Mapbox Studio provides us with all the typography that we should need. It comes bundled with 300 professional quality fonts to use on the maps.

 Fonts are provided free of charge for exclusive use in maps with Mapbox Studio. It's actually not allowed to use them in any other case.

What about exporting high-resolution images to print? Mapbox Studio has the capability to export images up to 600 dpi with one click:

Now, we have come to a point where you may ask, "what's the catch?"

Using Mapbox Studio is not free; it's a paid service. There is a starter plan offered by Mapbox, which is free, but it's very limited in what you can do with it. Mapbox plans are based mainly on map views, storage, and the custom styles you can host.

The starter plan at the time of writing this book, apart from allowing 3,000 views per month and 100 MB storage, has just one custom style, which means that we cannot have more than one custom dataset overlaid on our vector maps. Luckily, Mapbox introduced a basic plan for just $5 per month, which offers three styles, 1 GB storage, and 10,000 views per month, so anyone can now start working with it without being limited. A while ago, Mapbox had a standard plan for $49 per month. While this was not a showstopper if you planned to use what Mapbox offers professionally, it was for people who just wanted to explore Mapbox Studio's capabilities.

By this time, you may be thinking that if Mapbox Studio and other Mapbox technologies are currently open source, what stops us from hosting the maps in our own servers? Well, nothing stops us, but deploying the whole Mapbox stack to our own server is *extremely complicated* and beyond most people's skills.

Introducing CartoCSS

The time has come to explain how we can fully customize our maps to create the style we want.

CartoCSS is a powerful stylesheet-like language powering TileMill and Mapbox. It's extremely powerful and only limited by our imagination. If you are familiar with CSS for the Web, you will feel right at home when you start working with CartoCSS. If you have never developed for the Web, don't worry at all. Learning CartoCSS is extremely easy and fun.

Let's begin by explaining how it works.

How CartoCSS works

CartoCSS, like CSS, is based on selectors. A selector, for example, can be an ID of a specific layer, a zoom range, or a layer class. An ID may be called `#roads`, which means that whatever attributes we change within the closures will only affect roads.

Once we have our selector defined, we have to specify which attributes we want to modify in this context. For example, we may want to change the street outlines to a different color, so the attribute in this case is `line-color`.

Let's consider an example selector in action:

```
#sf-lines[highway="motorway"] {
  line-width: 5;
}
```

Now, let's dissect this example.

`#sf-lines` is the name of the layer. We can name the layers at the time we import them into TileMill *however we want*.

In the square brackets, there is `[highway="motorway"]`, which means that we want to find the `highway` feature in this layer and select all the motorways.

Within the curly brackets (which are called closures) is what we want to modify. In this example, it's all the motorways in the `sf-lines` layer.

> The `line-width: 5` part of the code means that we want to set the line width to 5 pixels.

Have a look at the following screenshot:

Observe the `#sf-lines` layer name in the **Layers** management dialog in the lower-left corner of the screen.

Certain attributes can only be applied to a specific type—which are called **symbolizers**—for example, `line-width` and `line-color`. These refer to the thicknesses and colors of lines and can obviously be applied to lines only, while others, such as `fill-color`, can only be applied to polygons.

The style types are called symbolizers in the Mapbox language (which originates from **Mapnik**, a technology used to render maps).

There are currently 10 symbolizers in TileMill, and each one can be applied to a certain type of geometry. The symbolizers are as follows:

- Line (lines and polygons)
- Polygon (polygons only)
- Point (points only)
- Text (points, lines, and polygons)
- Shield (points and lines)

- Line pattern (polygons)
- Raster (rasters)
- Marker (points, lines, and polygons)
- Buildings

We can repeat this process to specify as many selectors as we want, and in each one, we can change as many parameters as we want.

Filters

CartoCSS allows us to use filters in order to specify ranges; for example, we can use the `[zoom = 10]` filter to apply styling only at zoom level 10.

Let's consider an example of how we can use zoom filters:

```
[zoom < 16] {
  #sf-lines[highway="primary"] {
    line-width: 3;
  }
}
```

In this example, the first selector is `zoom < 16`, which means only the instances when the zoom is less than 16. From the `#sf-lines` layer, we select all the primary roads. Then we set `line-width` to 3.

In the preceding example, we used zoom to adjust the line width of the roads. As you may have noticed in various mapping services, maps usually display less detail as you zoom out, which happens because they don't want to overwhelm the user by displaying information that does not make sense at these zoom levels.

Imagine a map of the United States zoomed out to a level where every state is visible on the screen. What would happen if we were to display, at this specific zoom level, every street name down to the smallest walk path?

Comparisons

As you may have noticed in the preceding section, we used comparison filters to specify the criteria. We have already used `highway="motorway"`, which is a text filter, and `[zoom < 16]`, which is a zoom level filter.

Let's take a look at some more examples to understand the power of filtering our content.

For zoom level filters, we can limit the zoom levels to a specific range using the following code:

```
#sf-lines[zoom=>5][zoom<=12]
```

This simply means the instances when the zoom is *between* 5 and 12.

We can do the same using numeric filters. Here's an example:

```
#earthquakes[magnitude > 4][magnitude < 7]
```

Here, from the `earthquakes` layer, we are selecting the points *between* magnitudes 5 and 6. Note that the equals sign is missing.

For text comparisons, we can use the following code:

```
#sf-lines[highway != "primary"]
```

From the `#sf-lines` layer, select everything *except* primary highways. Alternatively, you can use the `=~` operator to specify a regular expression, as follows:

```
#sf-lines[highway =~ ".* Highway"]
```

In the preceding example, *both* major and secondary highways will be selected.

Working with colors

We can define a color by directly setting the value next to the property, as follows:

```
background-color: #b5e3ff
```

This will set the background color to blue. The color value is represented in hex.

To simplify our work and have an easier time when tweaking or fine-tuning our design, CartoCSS allows us to use variables to define colors (and many other values), as follows:

```
@water: #b5e3ff;

Map {
  background-color: @water;
}

Water {
  fill-color: @water;
}
```

At the beginning, we defined a variable called `@water` with a hex value of `#b5e3ff`. We set this variable as the color value for both the background and the fill color of water. This will save us from replacing multiple values within the editor when we need to make a change.

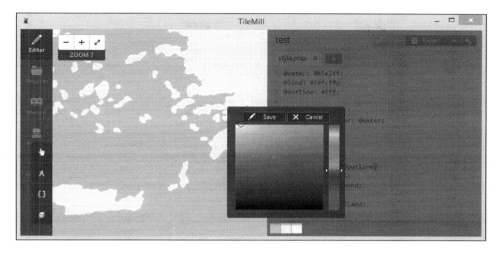

In the TileMill editor, colors are also represented with a color swatch directly below the text. You can simply click on the swatch, a color palette will appear, and you can select a color you like.

Styling lines

Let's explore some common techniques of styling lines.

The attributes we already know for lines are `line-color` and `line-width`. Another useful attribute is `line-join`. It changes how lines appear at the points where they join other lines.

Let's consider an example of how it looks if we don't set this attribute at all, which means that it uses the default `line-join` parameter, `miter`:

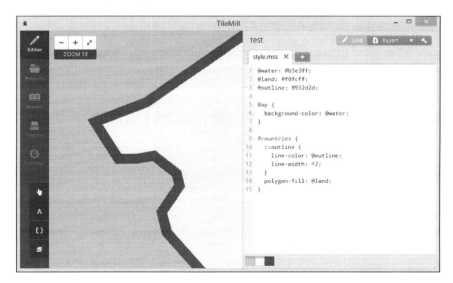

Now, we will set `line-join: round`:

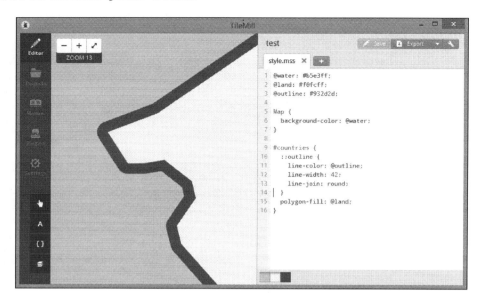

You can also try setting it to `bevel` and spot the differences as compared with the preceding screenshots.

Another useful parameter is `line-cap`, which sets how lines look at the ends. You can set it to `butt` (default), `round`, and `square`:

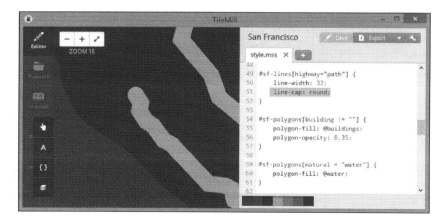

The `line-dasharray` property can take a comma-separated list of pixel widths as a value. Each value represents a dash and a space in this order. For example, `line-dasharray: 24, 12` will create a dash of 24 pixels and a space of 12 pixels.

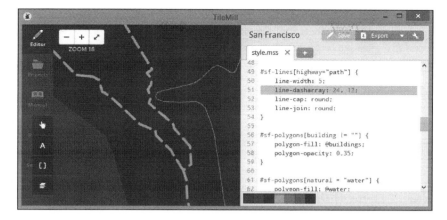

 You can set as many values as you like to create more complex styles; for example, `line-dasharray: 24, 12, 15, 7, 12, 3` is perfectly valid.

Note that we combined `line-dasharray` with `line-cap` and `line-join` to get the rounded look.

Styling polygons

Polygons are filled areas. We usually style them with a solid color or pattern. Polygons can also be styled with the attributes that we saw before, such as `line-width` and `line-color`, but let's explore some new ones that work specifically for polygons.

The most common one is `polygon-fill`. It simply fills the polygon with a solid color. Take a look at the following code:

```
#countries {
  polygon-fill: #aaa;
}
```

We can specify the opacity of the polygon using the `polygon-opacity` attribute, as follows:

```
#countries {
  polygon-fill: #aaa;
  polygon-opacity: 0.50;
}
```

 If a layer is opaque, the layer behind it becomes visible. If there is no layer behind it, the background color becomes visible.

We can fill a polygon using a texture or seamless pattern. We can also create our own patterns using image processing software, such as Photoshop or Gimp. Another option is to download patterns from a website such as `http://subtlepatterns.com` or `http://www.patterncooler.com/`.

We can define the pattern we want to use using the `polygon-pattern-file` style. It takes the URL of an image file as a parameter, as follows:

```
#countries {
  polygon-pattern-file:
    url("http://www.mysite.com/pattern01.png");
}
```

Have a look at the following screenshot:

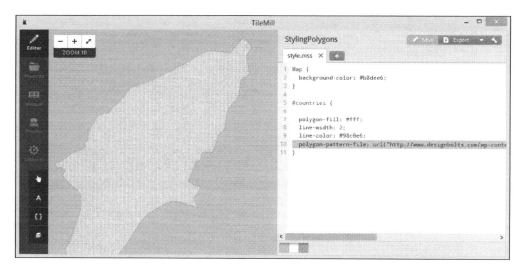

This pattern is only applied to the polygon that we defined within our selector. To apply patterns in the background, we can use the `background-image` property, as follows:

```
#countries {
  background-image: url("pattern01.png");
}
```

Styling labels

It's almost certain that at some point, we will need to style labels. By this, we mean how the text for road names, cities, or countries will look.

The most basic form of styling text can be found in the following example:

```
#countries {
    text-name: [NAME];
    text-face-name: 'Arial Bold;
}
```

First of all, we need to fetch text from our layer data. We can do this using `text-name:` `[NAME]`, where NAME is the attribute name of our layer.

We also need to specify `text-face-name`. This is the font name that will be used by TileMill to display the text on the screen. This is not the font filename but how the font is named internally. You can use the fonts browser within TileMill to browse the available fonts in your system and see their internal names.

We can change the text color using the `text-fill` property and the text size with the `text-size` property.

There is a property called `text-halo-fill`, which in simple words is the outline color of the font; however, in order for it to be visible, you have to also specify the `text-halo-radius` value with the radius in pixels.

A complete styled text will look similar to the following example:

```
#countries {
    text-name: [name];
    text-size: 16;
    text-fill: @text;
    text-face-name: "Arial Bold";
    text-halo-radius: 1;
    text-halo-fill: #AC8812;
}
```

Have a look at the following screenshot:

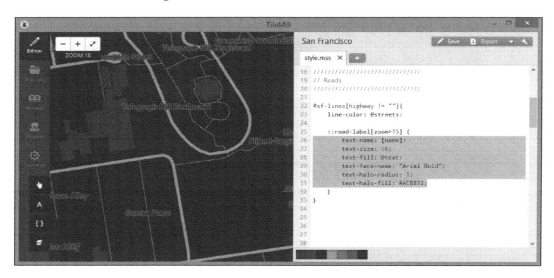

If we look at this screenshot, the street labels are not aligned with the streets. The map looks a bit weird because in many cases we can't tell which label belongs to which street. It would be much better if we could align the labels to the directions of the streets.

To do this, we can use the `text-placement` property. It takes four different parameters, but the most commonly used one is `line`, which aligns the label in the line's direction:

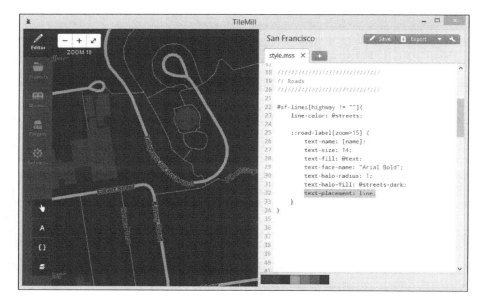

The complete selector can be found in the following example:

```
#countries {
    text-name: [name];
    text-size: 16;
    text-fill: @text;
    text-face-name: "Arial Bold";
    text-halo-radius: 1;
    text-halo-fill: #AC8812;
    text-placement: line;
}
```

Attachments

You may have noticed in the preceding screenshot that the selector contains another nested selector that starts with two double colons (: :). This type of selector is called **attachments**.

It's a way to instruct TileMill to *draw the same element again*, but this time, we will style it with the properties modified within the selector closures.

If we start using two double colons, we must specify a name. This name can be whatever we want; we can name it so as to remember what this attachment does. Then, in this context, we can specify any properties that we want to modify.

Let's consider an example:

```
#countries {
    line-color: #0000ff;
    line-width: 6;
    polygon-fill: #dd0000;

    ::second-outline {
        line-color: #ff0000;
        line-width: 3;
    }
}
```

In the preceding example, TileMill draws an outline of the #countries layer, with a width of 6 pixels and the color blue. Then, at : : second-outline, it draws the layer again, but this time with the color red and a width of 3 pixels.

As you can see in the following screenshot, it's a great way to generate glows and other types of effects; the best part of it all is that you can redraw the layer as many times as you want!

The power of CartoCSS lies in the concepts that we explained in the preceding section. By following these simple rules, you can transform your map to whatever you have in your imagination.

Styling a map with TileMill

If you haven't downloaded TileMill yet, head over to the Mapbox website and download it right now from `https://www.mapbox.com/tilemill/`.

The installation is pretty straightforward, and detailed instructions are provided in the page you download TileMill from, for all supported operating systems—Windows, OS X, and Linux.

How it works...

Once TileMill is installed and you have opened it, you will be greeted with the templates screen, where you can select one of the predefined templates, one of your previous projects, or create a new one:

Go ahead and select any template you like. We will examine the user interface at this point.

After a template is selected, we will consider the main user interface of TileMill. It is separated into different sections, with the most dominant section being our styled map:

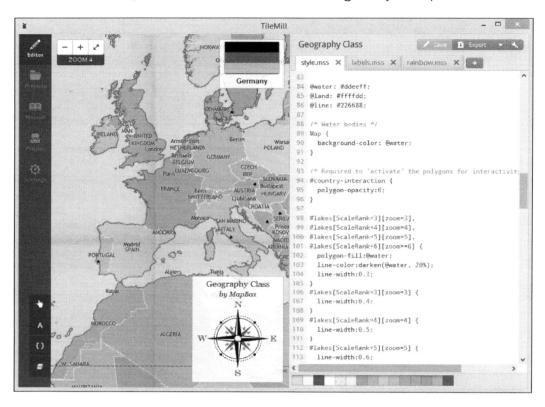

The map will be a live preview, showing the data that we imported into TileMill.

At this point, it is worth mentioning again that TileMill *is not connected to any mapping service* and does not fetch live map data. What we see in the map is the data that we (or the template) imported into TileMill.

In an ideal situation, we could open TileMill, zoom to a region of our choice, and be able to see and style all the features, such as the roads and the buildings. Sadly, however, this is not the case. What we import is what TileMill displays and allows us to style. Remember that it displays the changes after we save the project, not at the moment that the import is completed.

In the preceding screenshot, on the right-hand side is the CartoCSS editor, which displays a huge chunk of code. Don't be afraid; once we understand how CartoCSS works, parsing and understanding this code will be a piece of cake. CartoCSS is not as complex as a full object-oriented language. It's a matter of understanding some basic concepts and rules, that's all.

On the left-hand side of the screen, you will see a dark gray area with some buttons aligned vertically. Let's check them out one by one:

▶ **Editor**: This is the first button; it brings you to the exact screen that you are currently looking at.

▶ **Projects**: This is the screen you saw when you first started TileMill. It is where you select a template or your own project.

▶ **Manual**: This is just a quick reference explaining the main functionality of TileMill.

▶ **Plugins**: This allows you to download plugins with extra functionality, which will be integrated directly into Mapbox.

▶ **Settings**: This is where we set up everything ranging from where your projects are saved, autoupdates, and other aspects of the application.

Let's head back to the **Editor** tab. In the lower-left corner of the screen, we will find another group of buttons—the Editing Tools. Let's start exploring them:

▶ **Templates** is the first button. Here, we can define various aspects of the map that we are styling.

The first option allows us to set up a legend, and we can use HTML and inline CSS to design our legend as we like. We can also set up a teaser that shows upon hovering or when tapping on a mobile device. Next, there is a full description tab, and in the end, we can set up the location to which we can also add a link:

▶ **Fonts** is the next button. TileMill opens a window and displays the full list of fonts installed in the system. Using this section, you can easily copy the font name and paste it into the editor. It's kind of hard to remember the full font name, so this section is very helpful:

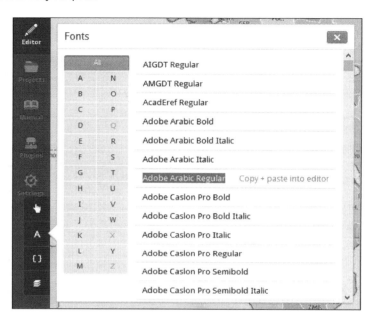

▶ After Fonts, you will notice an icon that looks like curly brackets. This is a reference to CartoCSS. This is the **Carto** button.

Do not underestimate this button! It will be your friend while learning CartoCSS! Especially at the beginning, remembering all CartoCSS parameters will be difficult. Do not be afraid to go into this section if you are looking for help:

- ▶ The last button is the **Layers** button. The most important functionality of TileMill lies here as it gives you access to layers.

  Each group of data that you import goes into a layer, and from this section, you can add, edit, or delete your layers. There is also a layer data inspector to view the layer data in a spreadsheet-like screen.

How to do it...

Perform the following steps:

1. Download, or generate using GIS software, the map data required for the map.
2. Create a new TileMill project by clicking on **New project**.
3. Go to the **Layers** palette, click on **Add Layer**, and import the data into TileMill.
4. Style the map using CartoCSS.

Downloading the map data

Before we begin with TileMill, let's get the data needed for this recipe. We will download data in an already extracted format. The data contains the shapefiles that we need to import into TileMill. Perform the following steps:

1. A well-known website to get extracted map data is `http://metro.teczno.com/`. Head over to this website now and select a city or region:

2. From the region of your choice, you will need two shapefiles. Download the `coastline` shapefile and the `osm2pgsql` shapefiles. The first one is only the coastline, and `osm2pgsql` shapefiles include everything else that we will need, such as roads, building labels, and other features.

   We have downloaded the San Francisco files for this example; if you want, you can follow our example, but it really doesn't matter. Any region will do just fine.

3. Extract the ZIP files in a folder of your choice.

4. Each ZIP file will extract several files with extensions such as `.dbf`, `.prj`, `.shx`, and `.shp`.

Inspecting the downloaded files using QGIS

You can totally skip this step and just import everything we downloaded directly into TileMill. However, I strongly suggest that you go through the process and learn how to inspect data.

TileMill shows the main attributes of the file in a spreadsheet-like form. We will use a free open source GIS software to explore the files in detail and the attributes that they contain. Perform the following steps:

1. **Quantum GIS (QGIS)** is an open source software that we can use if we want to take a look at what kind of data a shapefile contains. It's available for every major platform, and it's absolutely free, so go ahead and download it from `http://www.qgis.org/en/site/`.

   The installation instructions can be found on the QGIS website, and they are pretty simple. Go ahead and install it now.

   QGIS will install many applications, such as QGIS Desktop and QGIS Browser. We need to open QGIS Desktop.

2. Go to the **Layer** menu, click on **Add Layer**, and then on **Add Vector File**. A dialog will come up. Ensure that the **Source type** is **File** and then click on the **Browse** button to choose a `.shp` file. I picked `san-francisco.osm-line.shp`:

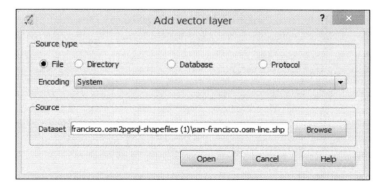

3. Click on **Open** to import the layer into QGIS:

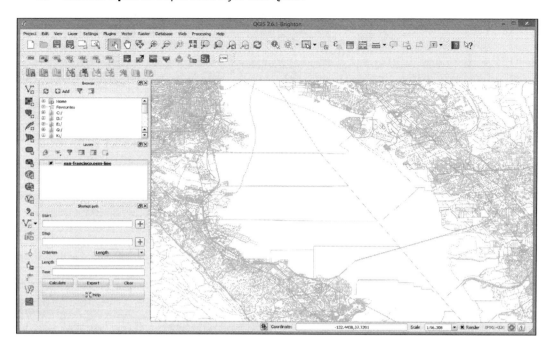

I will not go into a detailed explanation of how QGIS works, as it could be a book of its own. For the purpose of this recipe, we just need to know how to navigate the map.

Clicking and dragging on the map area scrolls the map. We can use the scroll wheel to zoom in or out.

4. Click on the Open Attribute Editor icon in the toolbar. This will open a spreadsheet-type editor, which displays all the attributes contained in this shapefile:

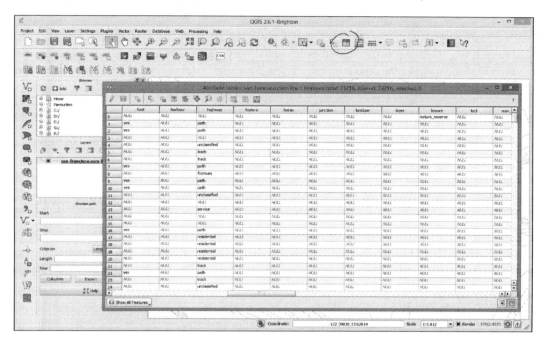

5. Observe the attributes, such as **highway**. We can see that it contains values such as **footway**, **path**, **residential**, and so on. These are the attributes and values that we will use in TileMill to style our map.

6. On the **Attribute table**, click on the Select Features Using an Expression button. The **Select by expression** dialog box will pop up:

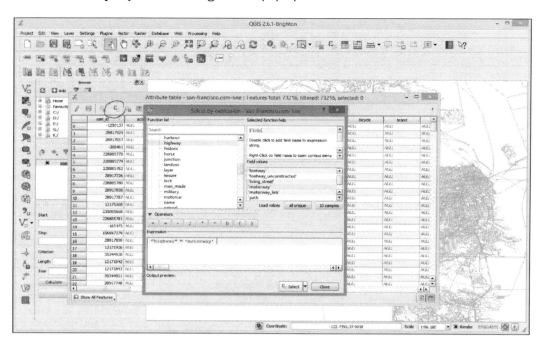

7. In this dialog box, we can select the values we want in two ways. The first option is to type the expression directly in the **Expression** section at the bottom of the screen.

   The second option is to select the **Fields and Values** category in the **Function list** section on the left-hand side and then double-click on the attribute that you are interested in—for example, **highway**. Note that the attribute appears in the expression section at the bottom.

8. Next, select the equals (=) sign from **Operators**.

9. Click on the **all unique** button for **Load values**. All the values of the selected attribute column will appear in the **Field values** list.

10. Double-click on the value (for example, **motorway**). The expression editor will display **"highway" = 'motorway'**.

11. Finally, click on the **Select** button and then on **Close** to close the dialog.

12. If you scroll to the attribute editor, you will notice that some rows are now selected; these are all the rows where the highway attribute is equal to motorway. To view the motorways highlighted in the map, click on the Zoom Map to the Selected Rows button in the attribute editor toolbar. It's the one that looks like a magnifier. You can also press *Ctrl + J* in Windows and Linux or *Cmd + J* on Mac.

13. Close the attribute editor, and you will see all the motorways highlighted in the map.

In case you do not understand what an attribute or value represents, head over to http://wiki.openstreetmap.org/ and type the attribute or value in the search box on the upper right-hand side. For example, you can see all the values of the highway attribute that we just explored at http://wiki.openstreetmap.org/wiki/Key:highway.

You have now learned a powerful way to inspect shapefiles and their attributes. If you are in the GIS business, you probably already have this skill. If you are just a developer with the ultimate purpose of creating the most beautiful maps in the world, then you may have never encountered GIS software before.

I strongly encourage you to learn how to use QGIS or any other GIS software in this case. There are many times that you may receive data from other sources in a non-standard format with unknown attributes.

Without this type of software, it is *extremely difficult* to find which attribute represents which feature on the map. Not having the capability to visualize shapefiles and find out what features they contain is a huge drawback.

Importing downloaded data into TileMill

It's time to create a new project and import the data we downloaded earlier from the Metro Extracts website into TileMill:

1. Fire up TileMill. You will be greeted with the **Projects** screen, where you can choose one of the templates that come with TileMill, a previous project, or create a new project.

2. Click on the **New project** button, and we will start from scratch.

3. In the **New project** dialog box, type any filename you want. The **Name** and **Description** fields are optional. Ensure that the **Image Format** is PNG (24-bit).

4. Leave the **Default data** checkbox selected. This will import a world layer into the project automatically. We don't need it, but it will help us to navigate, and we can always get rid of it later.

5. To close the dialog box and create our new project, click on the **Add** button.

6. Great! We are now into TileMill. You will see the world layer that we imported earlier when creating the project. There is one style currently active—`style.mss`—which is the one that gives the current map the blue background color representing the sea. The countries are styled with `line-color` specified as a darker blue and `line-width` of 2, and they are filled with a pure white using `polygon-fill`:

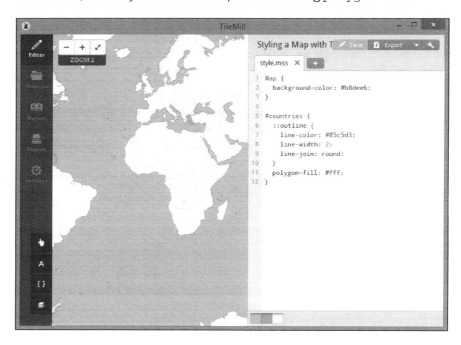

7. Open **Layers**. You will see the `#countries` layer that was imported by TileMill automatically. Leave it for now, and click on the **Add layer** button to add a new layer:

8. In the **Add layer** dialog box, select **Browse** and browse to the location of the extracted ZIP files. We will import the polygons first. My file is called `san-francisco.osm.polygon.shp`; yours may be different depending on the area that you download, but the filename will always end with `polygons.shp`.

9. Click on **Done** to browse the dialog box to return to **Add layer**. The next thing we will need to do is specify an ID. TileMill set mine as `sanfrancisco` automatically, but as I will import more layers, this ID won't make sense, and it's better to select something more appropriate. It will help us separate it from the lines and layers containing other datatypes. I will set my ID to **sf-polygons** for the San Francisco polygons. Finally, click on **Save**:

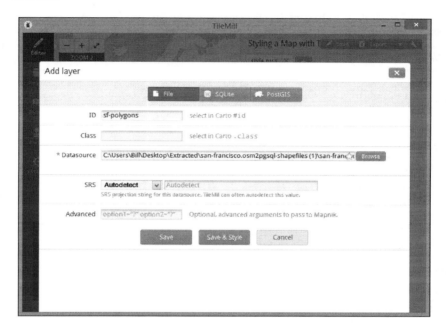

In most cases, you won't need to adjust the **SRS** field. However, in case it fails, we have to provide the correct value in this field.

Spatial Referencing System (**SRS**) is a quick way to identify a spatial referencing system using the PROJ.4 syntax. There are several ways to get the PROJ.4 string, but one of the easiest is by searching on `http://www.spatialreference.org/`.

You can find the PROJ.4 string for WGS 84 at `http://www.spatialreference.org/ref/epsg/4326/proj4/`, which is the following:

+proj=longlat +ellps=WGS84 +datum=WGS84 +no_defs

For more information regarding the PROJ.4 specification, visit `http://trac.osgeo.org/proj/`.

10. You will return to TileMill. Note that **#sf-polygons** is now in the **Layers** list. Click on the magnifier icon next to the **#sf-polygons** layer. The map will zoom in to the region that the data is located on.

11. Repeat the procedure and import the other two layers `san-francisco.osm-line.shp` and `san-francisco.shp` from the `coastlines` ZIP file. You can set up the IDs as `#sf-lines` and `#coast`, respectively.

12. The layer order is very important in TileMill, and if you import the layers in the order described previously, you will have the `#sf-polygons` layer at the bottom, `#sf-lines` in the middle, and `#coast` at the top. The layer order specifies the order that TileMill draws the layers in, and by this we mean that data may be covered by the layers above it. In this case, our lines, which include the roads, will be covered by the coastlines' polygons.

    Notice that the icon next to each layer shows what type of data it contains. It may show a line with two dots for line data and a filled polygon shape for polygon data.

    You can drag this icon to change the layer order. Try it now and set the layer order with `#coast` at the bottom, `#sf-lines` in the middle, and `#sf-polygons` at the top.

Styling data using CartoCSS

You need to perform the following steps:

1. First of all, let's set up our color palette. Clear the `style.mss` stylesheet of all code and copy the following variables:

    ```
    @water: #2f4145;
    @water-outline: #384C51;
    @land: #322f2e;
    @streets: #D7AE26;
    @streets-dark: #AC8812;
    @buildings: #6D6765;
    @text: #392C00;
    ```

    Well, you are looking at hex values, and it is kind of difficult to decipher the colors just by reading them.

    Luckily, TileMill displays the colors used in CartoCSS in the color swatches at the bottom of the screen. Clicking on a color swatch allows you to change this color using a handy color picker.

This is not the best way to build a color palette. Now is the perfect time to talk about the tools that can help us build a really beautiful color scheme. We want to design the most beautiful maps, after all!

One of the online tools we can use is Adobe Color (formerly, Adobe Kuler). You can access it at `https://color.adobe.com/`, and it will help you build your color scheme by selecting a color rule, such as monochromatic, complimentary, triadic, compound, or even building a custom color palette.

We can save our color scheme and share it with the Adobe Color community, as well as explore the color schemes designed by other people.

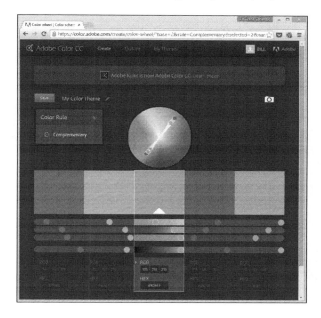

Another popular option is Paletton (`http://paletton.com`). It offers almost the same features as Adobe Color.

There is also Color Sphere! from MadCube, which is a Chrome extension, and there are even native applications such as ColorSchemer Studio 2 (`http://www.colorschemer.com/`).

2. Now, let's style the background and `#coast`, which is the coastlines shapefiles layer imported earlier. It's a polygon layer, and we will use `polygon-fill` and `line-color` to create a thin outline:

```
Map {
  background-color: @water;
}

#coast {
  polygon-fill: @land;
  line-color: @water-outline;
}
```

3. In order for TileMill to update the map, you will have to save, so ensure that you do this by clicking on the **Save** button on the upper right-hand side of TileMill:

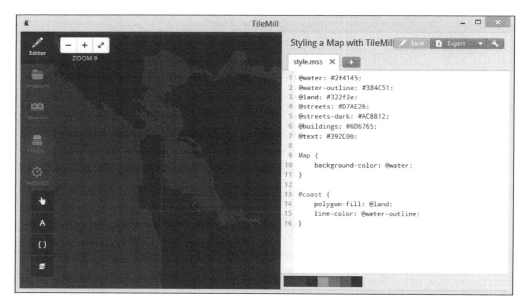

 The keyboard shortcut to save is *Ctrl* + *S* for Windows and *Cmd* + *S* for OS X.

At this point, we should be able to see the styled coastline. If nothing is visible, open **Layers** and click on the magnifier icon next to the coast. It will zoom to the region that the coastline is in.

Suppose you have an error in CartoCSS. In this case, TileMill will highlight the line number in yellow and display an error message at the bottom of the screen. Ensure that you fix all the errors and save again:

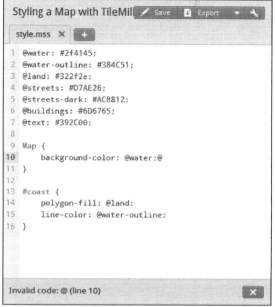

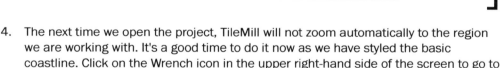

4. The next time we open the project, TileMill will not zoom automatically to the region we are working with. It's a good time to do it now as we have styled the basic coastline. Click on the Wrench icon in the upper right-hand side of the screen to go to **Project Settings**.

5. You will probably see a blank dark blue map. Our region is there, but we are currently at zoom level 1, and the whole world is visible. Using the zoom plus and minus buttons and dragging around the map, try to find the region that you are working with.

6. When you zoom in to the region, shift and drag to enclose it in a rectangle. This rectangle will define the area that we are working with and the one that TileMill will eventually export the tiles of.

7. Click on the center of the region, and a marker will appear. This is the center of our project.

8. When you have finished, click on **Save**:

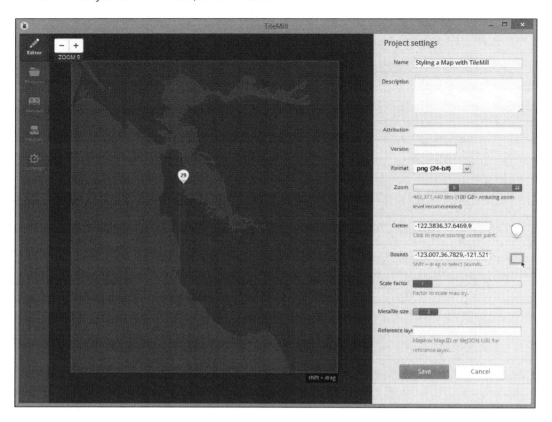

9. Back in the editor, let's style the roads. We will set the colors of all roads to yellow and then use different line widths for different types of roads by executing the following code:

```
// Set the colors of all roads to @street
#sf-lines[highway != ""]{
  line-color: @streets;
}

// for motorways, and trunk set line width to 5
#sf-lines[highway="motorway"],
#sf-lines[highway="trunk"] {
  line-width: 5;
}
```

```
// for primary roads, set line width to 3.
#sf-lines[highway="primary"] {
  line-width: 3;
}

// for secondary roads, set line width to 2
#sf-lines[highway="secondary"] {
  line-width: 2;
}

// for paths roads, set line width to 1, and use dashes
#sf-lines[highway="path"] {
  line-width: 1;
  line-dasharray: 5, 3;
  line-cap: round;
  line-join: round;
}
```

This is shown in the following screenshot:

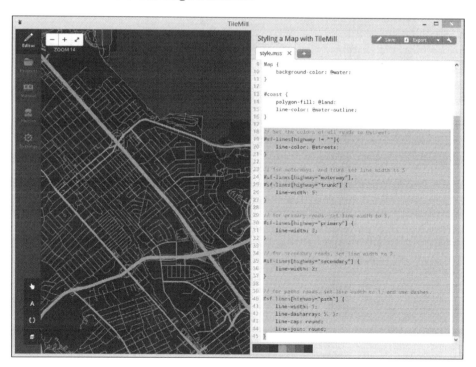

10. To style the buildings, we will fill them with the color that we defined in the variable and set the opacity to 0.35. This will mix the color of the buildings with the layer behind—in this case, the coastline. Run the following code:

```
#sf-polygons[building != ""] {
  polygon-fill: @buildings;
  polygon-opacity: 0.35;
}
```

In case you forget what features a layer contains, you can go to the **Layers** palette and click on the icon that looks like a spreadsheet next to the layer's name. TileMill displays a table with all the features of a layer and the values that they contain:

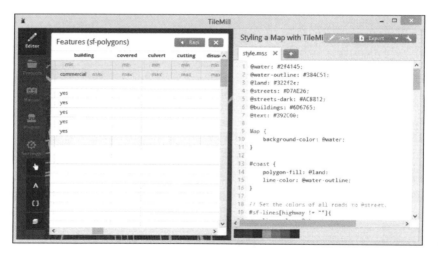

11. If you try to zoom out now, you will notice that the streets are very dense with a lot of detail at lower zoom levels. We will fix this next. Reduce the opacity of all roads to 0.45 when the zoom level is less than 16 through the following code:

```
[zoom < 16] {
  #sf-lines[highway != ""] {
    line-opacity: 0.45;
  }
}
```

12. Reduce the opacity of all roads to 0.25 when the zoom level is less than 14 with the following script:

```
[zoom < 14] {
  #sf-lines[highway != ""] {
    line-opacity: 0.25;
  }
}
```

13. Use this code to hide the roads when the zoom level is less than 12:

```
[zoom < 12] {
  #sf-lines[highway != ""] {
    line-opacity: 0;
  }
}
```

14. When the zoom level is less than 16, set the line opacity to 1 by executing the following code:

```
[zoom < 16] {
  #sf-lines[highway = "motorway"],
  #sf-lines[highway = "trunk"],
  #sf-lines[highway = "primary"],
  #sf-lines[highway = "secondary"], {
    line-opacity: 1;
  }
}
```

 Remember that styles at the bottom overwrite the ones above them. So, even if we set the opacity to 0.45 for zoom < 16 for all roads, motorways, trunks, and primary and secondary roads, they will still have an opacity of 1. The rest will remain at the previous value.

15. When the zoom level is greater than 15, you can use the following code:

```
[zoom > 15] {

  #sf-lines[highway="primary"] {
    line-width: 10;
  }

  #sf-lines[highway = "secondary"] {
    line-width: 8;
  }
```

```
  #sf-lines[highway = "tertiary"],
  #sf-lines[highway = "unclassified"],
  #sf-lines[highway = "residential"] {
    line-width: 6;
  }
}
```

Great! Try to zoom in and out now and you will notice the difference. Observe how the opacity of the roads reduces every time you zoom out and how certain features are hidden.

16. Our map already looks great, but it doesn't have labels yet. A map without road names will not be very popular! At the beginning of our style, directly below the #coast styling, we have a section that sets all road colors to street colors. Execute the following code:

```
#sf-lines[highway != ""]{
  line-color: @streets;
}
```

17. Let's add the label style in this selector. Replace CartoCSS in the preceding section with the following code. As we explained in the introduction, we forced TileMill to redraw the elements in the current selector with double colons :: (road-label is just a name we defined to remember what this redrawn part does). We will fetch road names from the [name] column. The rest of CartoCSS just consists of various typography attributes. We will also set text-placement to line, so the labels will be aligned with the lines of the roads:

```
#sf-lines[highway != ""]{
  line-color: @streets;

  ::road-label[zoom>15] {
    text-name: [name];
    text-size: 14;
    text-fill: @text;
    text-face-name: "Arial Bold";
    text-halo-radius: 1;
    text-halo-fill: @streets-dark;
    text-placement: line;
  }
}
```

This is how it will look:

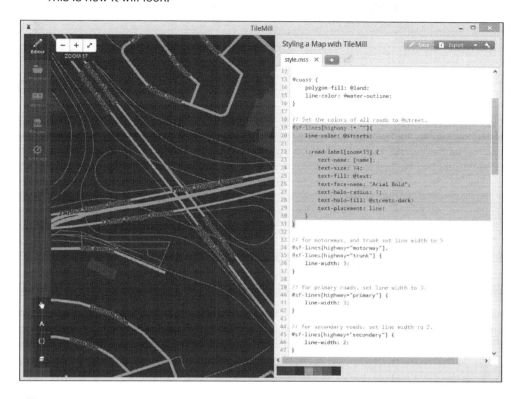

Styling a map with Mapbox Studio

In this recipe, we will style a map using Mapbox Studio. The biggest difference from TileMill is the workflow, while other parts, such as CartoCSS, remain the same.

How it works...

If you haven't installed Mapbox Studio yet, head over to the Mapbox website and download it now from `https://www.mapbox.com/mapbox-studio/`.

It's available for all major platforms, and the installation is pretty straightforward. Once installed, open the application and prepare for an interface tour!

When you first start Mapbox Studio, you will be greeted with the **Projects** screen, just as in TileMill.

You can start either by selecting a starter style (a template), or by creating a new style by selecting a source from the ones provided by Mapbox. The sources provided by Mapbox are Mapbox Streets, Mapbox Terrain, and Mapbox Satellite.

In case you want to overlay or import external data from other sources, you can create a new source by clicking on the **Blank Source** button on the right-hand side.

Once you have selected a style, you will be transferred to the style editor. The interface is separated into two parts, with the map on the left-hand side and the CartoCSS editor on the right-hand side, just as in TileMill:

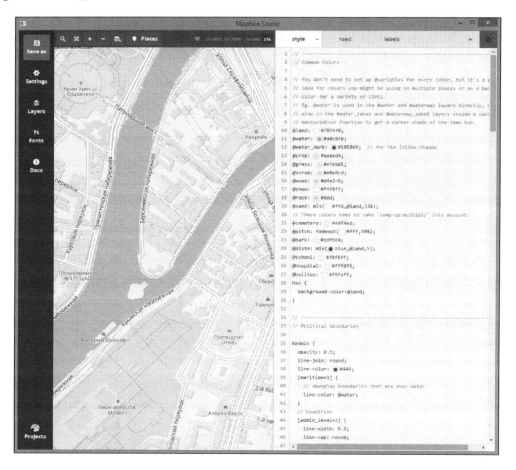

On the left-hand side, you will find the **Save as**, **Settings**, **Layers**, **Fonts**, and **Docs** buttons:

- ▶ **Save as**: This saves the project. You have to save each new project you create to your local hard drive.

- ▶ **Settings**: This allows you to configure the project settings, such as the available zoom levels and other parameters.

- ▶ **Layers**: This shows all the layers available at the source(s) that you select when you create the project.

- ▶ **Fonts**: This opens a window with a preview and the font names of the typefaces available for use in your maps.

- ▶ **Docs**: This opens a window with reference both to the user interface of Mapbox Studio and CartoCSS.

At the top of the window, there is a toolbar with some buttons. Let's check them out from left to right:

- ▶ **Search**: This allows you to search for a specific location on the map. Try a city or country to quickly jump to that location.

- ▶ **Full screen map**: This shows or hides the CartoCSS editor, showing the map in full screen.

- ▶ **+ and − buttons**: This zooms in or out of the map.

- ▶ **Inspector**: This allows you to visualize all layer data contained in the sources.

In the far upper-right corner of the CartoCSS window, you will find the Export Image button. It allows you to export images up to 600 ppi.

How to do it...

Perform the following steps:

1. Create a new project in Mapbox Studio by clicking on **Projects** and then on **+ New project**.

2. In the **New project** window, select the sources to be used in the map. The source could be one of the Mapbox ones, such as Mapbox Streets, Mapbox Terrain, or Mapbox Satellite, or a combination of them.

3. Style the map using CartoCSS.

Styling a map

Perform the following steps:

1. Create a new project in Mapbox Studio. We will not use a template; we will start from scratch. At the bottom of the **New projects** screen, you will see a **Create** button; next to it, ensure that it's **mapbox.mapbox-streets-v5**, which means that Mapbox Streets will be used as source.

   Remember, *we do not import data into Mapbox Studio as we do with TileMill*; instead, we will use the standard Mapbox sources provided to us. We can create our own sources if we want, and we can combine multiple sources together to create more complex maps.

   For now, we will use just Mapbox Streets, so click on the **Create** button:

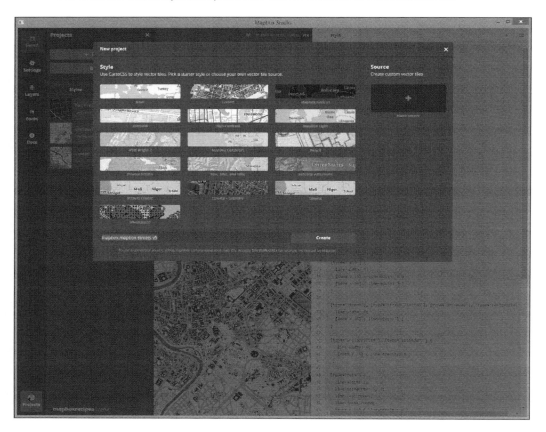

2. The editor will pop up with some basic imported CartoCSS. The first thing you will notice is that the **Save as** button in the upper-right corner is highlighted in blue. This means that the project is unsaved. We won't get far without saving, so let's do it right now.

Click on the **Save as** button, select a location on your hard drive, name the project as you want, and click on **Save**.

3. Zoom in to a region of your choice and clean up all the CartoCSS from the style. Hit **Save** again (*Ctrl* + S for Windows and *Cmd* + S for Mac). You will notice that the map is now blank. Don't worry, there is an awesome way to visualize data in Mapbox Studio.

4. Let's finish with the project setup first before we do this. Head over to **Settings** and increase **Maxzoom** to **22**.

5. Among the icons arranged on the topmost bar above the map is the Inspector icon. It looks like layers with a magnifier on top. Click on it now.

   The map now shows the data that the layer contains. If your zoom range is below 15, the data may be dense, so ensure that you zoom in until you get a clear picture of what's going on.

   If you click on various lines, you will see that a popup appears, showing you information such as the kind of layer, class, type, and name:

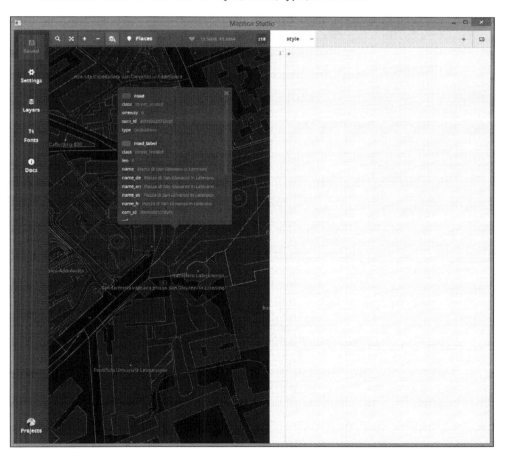

6. Let's define some colors. At the beginning of the style, add the following variables:

```
@water: #046380;
@some: #002F2F;
@land: #E6E2AF;
@outlines: #EFECCA;
@text: #A7A37E;
@green: #002F2B;
```

7. Open **Layers** from the Mapbox Studio sidebar. You will see all the layer IDs available in Mapbox Streets as we are using this source. Click on a layer ID to see what classes it has; for example, click on **#road**, and you will see that it can be one of **motorway**, **motorway link**, **main**, **street**, and so on.

8. We will begin by styling #water. First of all, set the background-color value, which in this case actually represents the ground color, then style #water. Run the following code:

```
Map {
  background-color: @land;
}

#water {
  polygon-fill: @water;
  line-width: 1;
  line-color: @outlines;
}
```

9. Click on **Save** when you have finished and inspect the map:

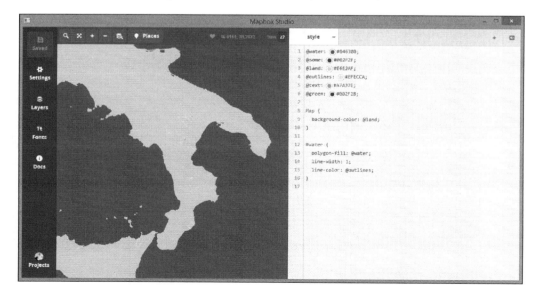

10. Continue inspecting the layers and styling the IDs that you need one-by-one in the same way that we did in TileMill. Here is the code for the complete style:

```
@water: #046380;
@some: #002F2F;
@land: #E6E2AF;
@outlines: #EFECCA;
@text: #A7A37E;
@green: #002F2B;

Map {
  background-color: @land;
}

#water {
  polygon-fill: @water;
  line-width: 1;
  line-color: @outlines;
}

//////////////////
/// ROADS ///
//////////////////

#road {

  line-color: @text;

  [type='motorway'], [type='motorway_link'] {
    line-width: 6;
    [zoom > 16] { line-width: 12 }
    [zoom < 14] { line-width: 3 }
  }

  [type='main'] {
    line-width: 5;
    [zoom > 16] { line-width: 8 }
    [zoom < 14] { line-width: 3 }
  }
```

```
      [type='street'], [type='street_limited'],
        [type='driveway'], [type='residential'] {
        line-width: 4;
        [zoom < 14] { line-width: 1 }
      }

      [type='unclassified'], [type='secondary'] {
         line-width: 4;
         [zoom < 14] { line-opacity: 0 }
       }

      [type="path"] {
        line-width: 1;
        line-dasharray: 5, 3;
        line-cap: round;
        line-join: round;
        [zoom < 16] { line-opacity: 0 }
      }
    }

    #road_label {
      text-name: [name];
      text-size: 18;
      text-fill: @text;
      text-face-name: "Meta Offc Pro Bold";
      text-halo-radius: 2;
      text-halo-fill: @land;
      text-placement: line;
    }

    /////////////////
    /// BUILDINGS ///
    /////////////////

    #building {
      polygon-fill: @green;
      [zoom < 13] {
        polygon-opacity: 0.0;
      }

    }
```

Here's the final result:

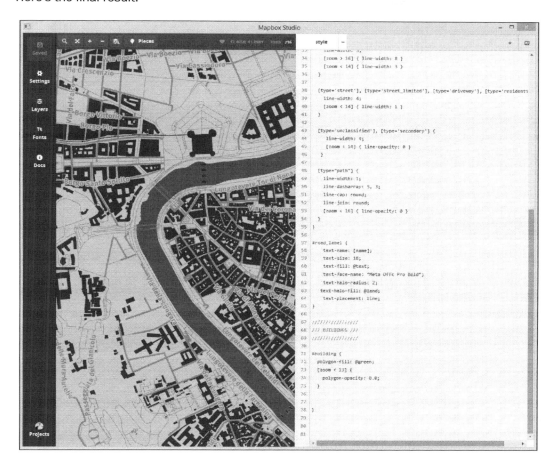

There's more...

In the previous section, you learned how you can use and style data provided by Mapbox.

Now, we will continue from there and take a look at how to *import our own data* into Mapbox Studio.

Perform the following steps:

1. Open Mapbox Studio. Click on **Styles & Sources** in the lower-left corner. We will need to create our own source. Click on **+ New Style or Source** at the top of the sidebar that opens up. On the left-hand side of the **New Style or Source** window, there is a **Source** section. Click on the **Blank source** button:

2. Now, we need to add our layers. The data that a layer can contain can be a shapefile; can be in the `.kml`, `.geojson`, `.gpx`, `.csv`, `.tif`, and `.vrt` formats; or can even be PostGIS and SQLite databases.

    We will use a shapefile that contains the national parks in US. You can download the file from `http://www.naturalearthdata.com/downloads/10m-cultural-vectors/parks-and-protected-lands/`. It's a ZIP file, so we will need to extract it somewhere on the hard drive.

3. Back in Mapbox Studio, click on the **Browse** button in the **Add a New Datasource** window, and select **ne_10m_parks_and_protected_lands_area.shp** from the files that we extracted in the previous step.

You will see that the shapefile has been imported correctly. Mapbox Studio now shows us a preview, and we can already zoom and pan. You can even click on a shape and a popup with the layer attributes will appear:

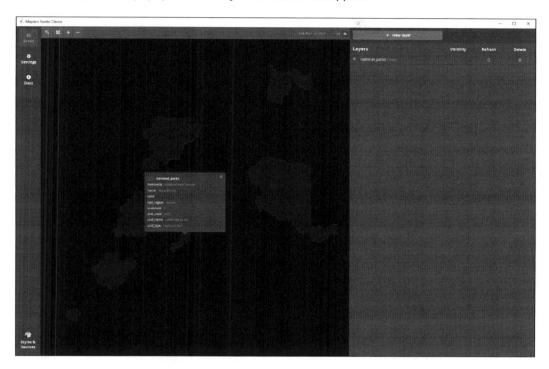

On the sidebar to the right, note that it correctly detected the projection and showed it in PROJ.4, which is as follows:

+proj=longlat +ellps=WGS84 +datum=WGS84 +no_defs

 You can add as many layers as you want in a single source and even a mix of shapes, GeoJSON, and other file types.

4. You can rename the layer if you want. Click on the **Rename** button below the filename at the top of the sidebar to the right. I named mine `national_parks` for simplicity.

5. Before uploading our own data to Mapbox, we need to save the project locally. Press *Ctrl + S* on Windows or *Cmd + S* on OS X, choose a filename, and store it somewhere on your hard drive.

6. Now that the project is saved, click on **Settings** and then on **Upload to Mapbox**. Mapbox Studio will initiate the process to upload the data to your Mapbox account.

7. Once the upload is completed, you can find the Map ID above the **Upload to Mapbox** button. Copy the Map ID; we will need it in a while.

8. That's all that's needed to create a new data source to be used in Mapbox Studio. Now, we need to open the map from the previous recipe. If you didn't complete the previous recipe, any of the sample projects will do just fine.

9. Once the project is open, click on **Layers** and then on **Change Source**. In the **Sources** window, before the **Apply** button is the source that we will use for this map, which is **mapbox.mapbox-streets-v5**.

10. We will need to append our own source, which we just created. We have the Map ID already copied to the clipboard, so add a comma (,) and paste the Map ID. The complete string should look similar to the following:

    mapbox.mapbox-streets-v5, mapboxrecipes.62340c1c

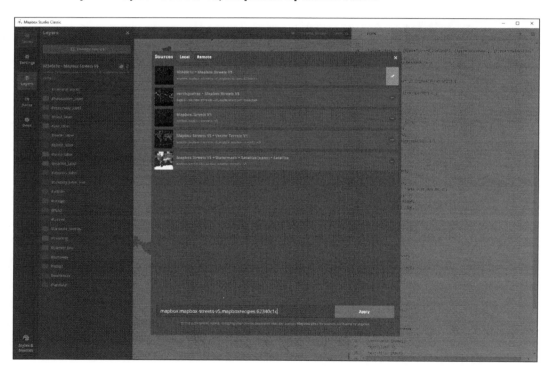

11. Click on **Apply**. Our own custom datasource will be added to the project.

    You can make sure of this by opening the **Layers** palette. Note that there is a **#national_parks** layer here. This is our own data source—the layer that we added earlier.

12. In order to see the layer, we need to style it first. For this layer, paste the following CartoCSS code at the bottom of the style:

```
#national_parks {
  polygon-fill: @green;
  opacity: 0.5;
  text-name: [name];
  text-size: 32;
  text-fill: @text;
  text-face-name: "Meta Offc Pro Bold";
  text-halo-radius: 2;
  text-avoid-edges: true;
  text-halo-fill: @green;
  [zoom < 7] {
    text-size: 18;
  }
}
```

13. Save the project and enjoy our custom data overlaid on the Mapbox Street map data:

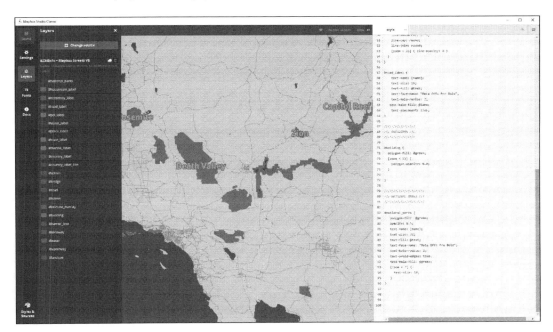

Publishing your base map on your server with PHP

So far, we have successfully used the tools provided by Mapbox to style our maps. We have also seen how easy it is to publish a map to the Mapbox platform, especially if we use Mapbox Studio.

There are cases where we may need to host a map on our own server, and we will explore two different ways of doing this.

In the first case, we will use PHP. While this is not the best option for this task, PHP can be found installed on *every server*, and projects using PHP are easy to deploy.

How it works...

First of all, we will export our maps from TileMill. The format that we will export in will be .mbtiles, which is actually a SQLite file containing the data and the tiles.

MBTiles is just a SQLite database that contains metadata information along with PNG images. Its purpose is to have a single file that contains everything needed to serve a map. In cases such as mobile applications, storing thousands of tiles and metadata information in the app container can be difficult to manage and can be extremely poor in performance.

The following is a screenshot showing the tables of the SQLite database along with the table of PNG files:

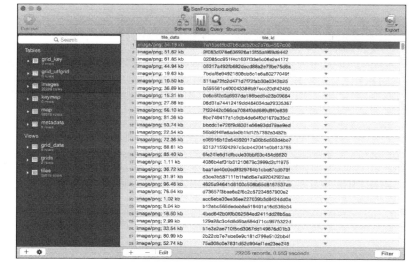

Reading SQLite files directly in PHP is not performant at all, so we will use **MBUtil** to convert them into PNG files. Next, we will use a PHP tile server developed by Petr Pridal. Developing our own tile server is not a hard task, but it is beyond the scope of this book. Finally, we will set up a simple project and serve the tiles.

How to do it...

Perform the following steps:

1. Export MBTiles from TileMill by clicking on **Export** and choosing **MBTiles** as the export option.

2. In **Export Options**, ensure that the zoom is configured and the center is within the bounds of our map.

3. Click on **Export**, and once finished, click on **Save** to store MBTiles on the hard drive.

4. Convert the MBTiles (SQLite) files into regular PNG files using MBUtil.

5. Use one of the open source tile servers, such as the PHP tile server, to serve the newly generated PNG files.

Exporting a map from TileMill

The steps are as follows:

1. Fire up TileMill and open the project you want to export. In the upper-right corner, you will find an **Export** combo box. Select it and choose **MBTiles**.

2. Set up the region that you want to export by defending the bounding box in the map. Also, ensure that the center is a location within the region.

3. Configure the zoom range to export. You will notice that as you increase the zoom, the time and hard drive space required to export also dramatically increases:

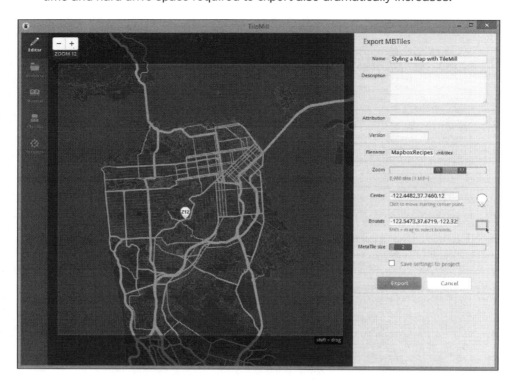

4. Click on **Export** to export your tiles. You will then be transferred to the export queue, and you will be able to monitor the progress and the time remaining:

5. Once finished, click on the **Save** button. TileMill will show you the location on your hard disk to find the exported MBTiles.

Converting an MBTiles database into regular PNG files

We will convert the MBTiles SQLite database into regular PNG files. The files have to follow a specific folder structure and a naming schema for us to be able to use them in the tile servers.

For the task, we will need an external utility called MBUtil. It's a powerful tool that allows us to specify our own naming scheme and even change the output format. In this case, the default XYZ naming scheme will do just fine, and the default format is PNG, which is exactly what we need.

Perform the following steps:

1. Let's download MBUtil. Head over to the repo and follow the instructions to set up MBUtil globally at `https://github.com/mapbox/mbutil`.

2. Once installed, convert your files using the `mb-util <inputfilename> <outputfolder>` command. A new directory will be created in the location you specified containing the tiles in an XYZ format.

> If you explore the folder exported by MBUtil, you will discover the file structure in the XYZ format:
>
>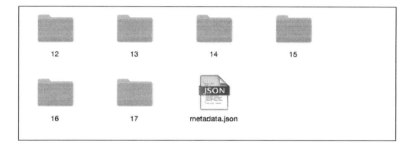
>
> It uses a folder for each zoom level, with each column being a subdirectory and each tile in the column a file. The other common format used in maps is TMS. You can read more about the XYZ format at `http://wiki.openstreetmap.org/wiki/Slippy_map_tilenames`.

Creating a tile server PHP project

We will download the PHP tile server developed by Petr Pridal, and we will set up a simple project that serves the tiles we exported in the previous recipe. Perform the following steps:

1. Create a new folder to host the project and get into it using the following command:

    ```
    mkdir MapBoxPHPServer && cd MapBoxPHPServer
    ```

2. We will use **tileserver-php**. It's extremely simple to use, and the whole project is just a single PHP file. Clone the project into the folder using the following command:

    ```
    git clone https://github.com/klokantech/tileserver-php
    ```

3. Now, copy the exported folder from MBUtil into the same directory as the `tileserver.php` file.

4. You can now access the `tileserver.php` file from a web browser at `http://localhost/tileserver.php`:

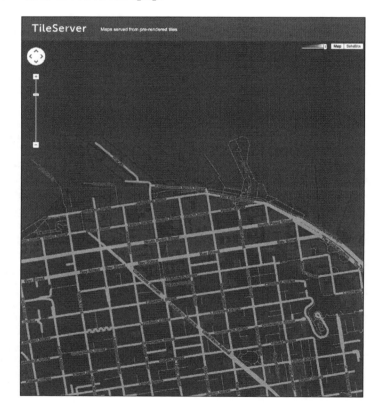

That's it! We can now serve our maps from our own PHP server. Deploying the server is extremely easy, and the only thing needed is to copy the files into the server. The best part is that PHP is installed almost everywhere, and it is also very easy to find a cheap hosting service.

Publishing your base map on your server with Node.js

As we explained in the previous chapter, PHP is not the ideal technology to use to serve our tiles. This is not because PHP is a bad language or anything similar; it's because there are other technologies that excel in multithreading operations, which is exactly what's needed when serving tiles at an enormous speed.

In this recipe, we will use **TileStream**, which is a high-performance tile server powered by MBTiles. TileStream is maintained by Mapbox and uses Node.js and SQLite as the backend technologies.

In the preceding PHP recipe, we converted the tiles to the XYZ format to squeeze out any performance benefits while serving the tiles. Node.js doesn't have any performance issues while reading the tiles directly from the MBTiles container, which is just a SQLite database, so we don't need to convert the tiles in this case.

We can use the MBTiles we exported in the previous recipe. Then we will download TileStream from GitHub, which is the tile server that we will use in this case.

Getting ready

TileStream requires Node.js v0.10.x or 0.8.x. It will *not work with the most recent versions* of Node.js, so ensure that you have one of the preceding versions installed.

If you don't have Node.js installed yet, go ahead and install it. Ensure that you do not install the latest build, but one of the versions required by TileStream.

How to do it...

Perform the following steps:

1. Export the MBTiles file from TileMill by clicking on **Export** and selecting **MBTiles** as the export option.

2. In **Export Options**, ensure that the zoom is configured and the center is within the bounds of our map.

3. Click on **Export**, and once finished, click on **Save** to store the MBTiles file on the hard drive.

4. Use any one of the open source Node.js tile servers, such as TileStream, to directly serve MBTiles.

Creating a tile server Node.js project

Perform the following steps:

1. Ensure that you have the correct version of Node.js installed. Open a terminal and type `node -version`, and Node.js will print out the version.

2. Start by creating a new folder in your hard drive. I named mine `MapBoxRecipes-NodeServer`.

3. Get into the folder and clone the TileStream repo using the following command:

   `git clone https://github.com/mapbox/tilestream.git .`

   The dot (.) at the end clones it into the folder that we are in without creating a new subfolder.

4. Once installed, ensure that the server is working. Start the TileStream server by typing `./index.js`.

5. Let's copy the `.mbtiles` file into a location that TileStream expects them to be in. The default directory is `~/documents/MapBox/tiles`.

6. Head over to a browser and type `http://localhost:8888/` to access TileStream. You can access the map of your choice directly using `http://localhost:8888/#!/map/SanFrancisco`:

That's it! We now have our custom MBTiles file exported from TileMill and served by our own Node.js server. You can use a hosting service that supports Node.js, such as Heroku, to deploy your project.

4
Mapbox.js

In this chapter, we will cover the following recipes:

- Creating a simple map
- Changing map properties programmatically
- Working with base layers
- Adding markers and popups
- Clustering markers to improve our map
- Getting mouse coordinates
- Working with controls
- Adding interactivity to your map with UTFGrid
- Creating a choropleth map
- Creating a heat map

Introduction

So far, we have investigated various ways to create and customize maps. At the beginning, we used the Mapbox user interface to create some simple styling on the maps, and then we explored recipes to utilize Mapbox services using PHP and Node.js. In the previous chapter, we also introduced CartoCSS, the stylesheet language that will help us to customize a map with absolute control.

None of the recipes, however, covered how to build dynamic maps and display features, such as markers, on the fly. This is what we will do in this chapter, and our backing technology is a JavaScript framework called **Mapbox.js**.

Mapbox.js inherits from another framework called **Leaflet**. Leaflet was created by Vladimir Agafonkin and various other contributors, and it's extremely popular and simple to integrate and use. It takes advantage of HTML5 and CSS3 in modern browsers but is also compatible with older ones.

Leaflet's features include covering, displaying, and overlaying layers and creating markers, popups, and vector layers. It's also capable of displaying GeoJSON data, image overlays, and WMS layers. It's currently advertised as a mobile-friendly JavaScript framework, and this is entirely true. It currently supports hardware acceleration on iOS, and it feels as smooth as a native app. Performance-wise, it is very lightweight (around 34 KB of gzipped JS code) and allows you to reduce the library size by excluding the features you don't want to use. It also doesn't require any external dependencies, which simplifies the integration even further. One of the advantages of Leaflet is the community support along with the myriad of plugins developed to cover almost any case.

Mapbox.js inherits from Leaflet, but we don't have to worry about this.

 Mapbox.js is a JavaScript framework. Basic knowledge of JavaScript will greatly help to understand the recipes in this chapter. Also, basic HTML5 and CSS skills are essential to be able to integrate the map into a webpage.

Creating a simple map

In this recipe, we will explore how we can integrate Mapbox.js into a project. We will use the absolute minimum code, and we will just display a simple map.

How to do it...

We have to create a simple HTML5 file that will include the necessary Mapbox.js JavaScript and CSS files.

We will also create our own CSS file to create some basic styling for our #map div that will contain the map. In main.js, we will initialize Mapbox.js and provide our Mapbox access token. Then, we will create a simple map by providing the basic coordinates. Perform the following steps:

1. Open up the chapter-4-example1-starter folder. This folder contains an HTML5 index.html file, a css folder with a style.css file, and a main.js file. The project isn't linked to Mapbox.js yet; we will do this next.

   The style.css file contains some basic styling for the #map div. It will style the div with 100% width and 800px height, with no margins. This div will contain our map.

   We will use main.js to write our JavaScript code and integrate Mapbox.js into the project.

2. Open `index.html` in your favorite editor. The files required are the `mapbox.js` file and the stylesheet `mapbox.css` file.

   Insert the following two lines inside `<head></head>` just before our `main.js` file:

```
<script src='https://api.tiles.mapbox.com/mapbox.js/
    v2.1.5/mapbox.js'></script>
<link href='https://api.tiles.mapbox.com/mapbox.js/
    v2.1.5/mapbox.css' rel='stylesheet' />
```

3. Now open `main.js`. You will see that we will initialize our map inside the `window.onload()` function. This function is triggered when the window in our browser is loaded.

   First, we will need to pass our access token, as follows:

```
L.mapbox.accessToken = 'pk.
eyJ1IjoibWFwYm94cmVjaXBlcyIsImEiOiJjd3RhQmlzIn0.
WxOfWGCo3gs6fzta5QrLfw';
```

   Here, `L` comes from Leaflet, and `.mapbox` is actually a reference to the Leaflet Mapbox plugin. You will notice that we frequently use either `L.mapbox` or `L` to refer to general Leaflet functions. Remember that Mapbox.js is just a Leaflet plugin.

4. Create a new variable called `mapboxTiles` and set up a tile layer using `L.tileLayer`, as follows:

```
var mapboxTiles = L.tileLayer('https://{s}.tiles.mapbox.com/v4/
mapboxrecipes.kk6jp52i/{z}/{x}/{y}.png?access_token=' + L.mapbox.
accessToken);
```

   We dissected the Mapbox URL format in previous chapters, but let's do it one more time:

   ❑ `/v4/`: This is the API version. Currently, the API is in version 4.

   ❑ `mapboxrecipes.kk6jp52i`: This is our Map ID.

   ❑ `/{z}/{x}/{y}.png`: This is the tile format. At the moment, we are using the XYZ `.png` format.

   ❑ `?access_token=' + L.mapbox.accessToken`: This indicates that we are passing our access token.

5. Next, let's add the layer we created to the map via the following code:

```
var map = L.map('map').addLayer(mapboxTiles).setView([42.3610,
-71.0587], 15);
```

   We get the map using (`'map'`), where `'map'` is our #map div. Then we add the layer we created earlier using `addLayer(mapboxTiles)`. Finally, we use `setView([42.3610, -71.0587], 15)` to set the coordinates and zoom levels.

6. Make sure that your modified `main.js` and `index.html` files are saved and then open `index.html` in a browser.

7. That's it! We just integrated Mapbox.js in an empty project, and we displayed a map in our #map div.

At this point, you will have already realized how simple it is to use JavaScript and Mapbox.js in your project. With a few lines of code, we were able to create a basic map and add it to the screen, as in the following screenshot:

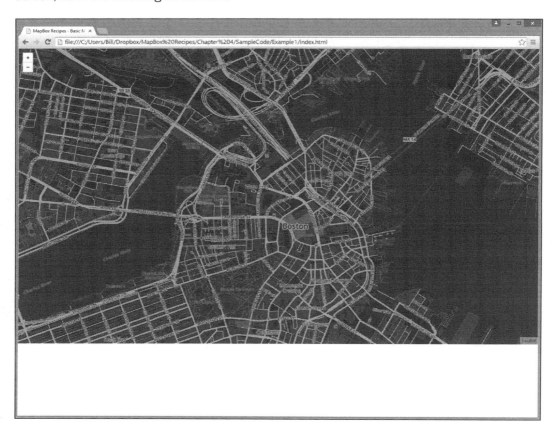

The completed project can be found in the `chapter-4-example1-completed` folder.

How it works...

The most important class of Mapbox.js is `L.map`. It's used to create a map on a page and manipulate it using various methods to modify the map state or listen for events such as clicks and mouseovers.

The map's core components are layers. You can create them dynamically, and there are different types of layers, such as base layers and feature layers. Overlaying various types of layers allows you to composite the final appearance of the map.

Changing map properties programmatically

Map properties are interaction handlers that allow you to customize how a user interacts with the map at runtime. You can enable or disable certain features, such as zoom, dragging, touch zoom, scroll wheel, and many more.

In this recipe, we will use our previous example and modify it to change the map properties programmatically.

You will learn how to change the zoom and center of the map, pan to specific coordinates or bounds, and restrict the movement to a region.

How to do it...

We will add a basic map with a base layer on the screen as in the previous recipe. Then we will use the `onClick` handler on various screen elements to trigger the `panTo` or `zoomIn` method in order to pan or zoom the map programmatically.

Panning the map programmatically

In this recipe, we will use the methods we discussed to change the map properties programmatically. Perform the following steps:

1. Open the `chapter-4-example2-starter` folder in your favorite text editor. The project is in exactly the same state as in the previous recipe.

    I added `<nav>` with the relative CSS to create the buttons in the upper-left corner. We will use these buttons to change the map properties programmatically.

2. Before the closing curly bracket in `window.onload()` and directly after `var map = L.map('map').addLayer(mapboxTiles).setView(latlong, 15)`, append the following code:

    ```
    map.getContainer().querySelector('#pan').onclick =
      function() {
      latlong[1] += 0.02;
      map.panTo(latlong, {animate: true, duration: 2.0});
    };
    ```

Let's take a look at how this code works. We will first call `getContainer()` to get the map container and then `querySelector('#pan')` to get the `<a href='#' id='pan'>Pan Right</a>` element from the HTML file. Then, we will attach an `onClick()` handler in it. The `onClick()` handler will perform the following actions each time the mouse button is clicked:

- It will increase the longitude in the `latlong` variable by `0.02` degrees.

- It will trigger `panTo()` and pass the new `latlong` variable along with some options, which in this case sets the `animate` parameter to `true` and the `duration` parameter to `2.0` seconds.

3. Open `index.html` in a web browser and click on the **Pan Right** button. The map will pan 0.02 degrees to the right each time the button is pressed.

Zooming the map programmatically

Perform the following steps:

1. Before the closing bracket in the `onLoad()` function, add the following code:

```
var zoomIn = true;

map.getContainer().querySelector('#zoom').onclick =
  function() {
  if (zoomIn) {
    map.zoomIn(2, {animate: true});
  } else {
    map.zoomOut(2, {animate: true});
  }
  zoomIn = !zoomIn;
};
```

2. Here, we will use the same `querySelector` method to get the `<a href='#' id='zoom'>Toggle Zoom</a>` button element from the HTML file.

The zoom in the `zoomIn(<Number> delta?, <zoom options> options?)` and `zoomOut(<Number> delta?, <zoom options> options?)` function is used to adjust the map zoom by two levels, as follows:

```
map.zoomIn(2, {animate: true});
```

Again, we will use `{animate: true}` as options to animate the zoom adjustment. The `<zoom options>` does not have a `duration` parameter.

3. Save the `main.js` file and open the `index.html` file in your browser. Click on the **Toggle Zoom** button and observe the results.

Zooming to a map region programmatically

Let's take a look at how we can zoom the map to Boston Airport using the `fitBounds()` method. Here are the steps that you need to perform:

1. At the end of the previous section's code, before the closing bracket in the `onLoad()` method, append the following code:

```
map.getContainer().querySelector('#fit').onclick =
  function() {
  var airportSW = [42.380261, -70.986013];
  var airportNE = [42.344492, -71.033392];
  var bounds = L.latLngBounds(airportSW, airportNE);
  map.fitBounds(bounds);
};
```

2. We will get the `#fit` element from the HTML file as before and generate a `bounds` variable using the following line of code:

```
latLngBounds(<LatLng> southWest, <LatLng> northEast)
```

We will pass the `airportSW` coordinate as the southwest part of the region and the `airportNE` variable as the northeast part.

Then we will use the `fitBounds()` method and pass the bounds we just created:

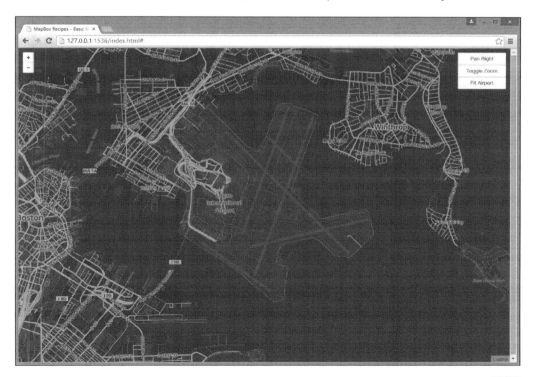

How it works...

In the previous recipe, we set the map view using the following method:

```
setView(<LatLng> center, <Number> zoom?, <zoom/pan options>
    options?)
```

In this method, we passed the coordinates and zoom level. It's important to know how to read the documentation. In the preceding example, the first parameter is `center`, and it expects a `<LatLng>`, which is the latitude and longitude. We can pass a simple array, as follows:

```
var latlong = [42.3610, -71.0587];
```

Alternatively, we can generate a `latlong` object and pass it instead, as follows:

```
var latlong = L.latLng(42.3610, -71.0587);
map.setView(latlong);
```

The next parameter is the `zoom`, and it expects a `<Number>`, but this one includes a question mark (?), which means that this parameter is optional and not required.

The same goes for the last parameter, `options`. In the specific method's option, we may pass `animate` to set whether the change is animated and the animation's duration using `duration`, as follows:

```
map.panTo(latlong, {animate: true, duration: 2.0});
```

Let's explore another property called `fitBounds`:

```
fitBounds(<LatLngBounds> bounds, <fitBounds options> options?)
```

This method is used to fit a specific region of the map on the screen. It will set the center and zoom to an appropriate value in order to fit the entire region on the screen.

A region, or bounds as it's called in Mapbox terminology, is a rectangle generated by two points: one in the southwest and one in the northeast, as shown in the following screenshot:

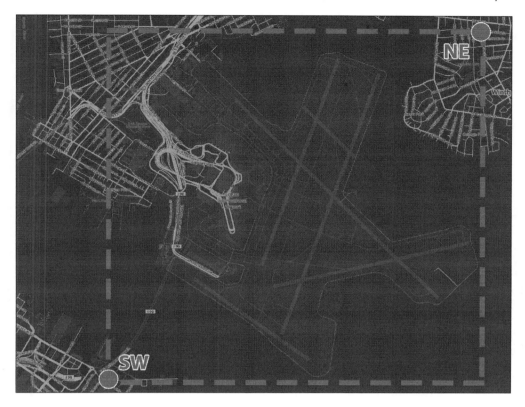

This method expects a `<LatLongBounds>`, which is a set of latitude and longitude coordinates. The first coordinate is to the northeast edge of the region, and the second is to the southwest edge, as follows:

```
var airportSW = [42.380261, -70.986013];
var airportNE = [42.344492, -71.033392];
```

At this point, you may pass the bounds directly as a simple array form, as you can note in the following code:

```
map.fitBounds([
    airportSW,
    airportNE
]);
```

Alternatively, you can generate a `bounds` object using the `latLngBounds` method and pass this instead, as follows:

```
var bounds = L.latLngBounds(airportSW, airportNE);
map.fitBounds(bounds);
```

Working with base layers

In this recipe, we will explore layers. Actually, we already added a base layer in the previous recipes using the `addLayer(<ILayer> layer)` method.

One of the advantages of the Mapbox API is the power to add multiple overlaid layers at runtime, which is an extremely useful feature that allows us to switch between different types of data without using a different map.

How to do it...

We will add a base layer on our map. This layer will be displayed when the page is displayed when first opening the browser.

Then, we will use `hasLayer(<ILayer> layer)` to check whether a layer is already on the map, and if not, we will add it with `addLayer(<ILayer> layer)`. In case a layer is already on the map, we will remove it first using `removeLayer(<ILayer> layer)`.

There are various types of layers. The first type is a base layer, which can display tiles from various sources, such as Mapbox Street, Mapbox Terrain, or Mapbox Satellite. The second type of layer is an overlay layer. Polygons, lines, and other shapes belong to this type of layer. The third layer is again an overlay layer, but it contains other features, such as markers.

In Mapbox, layers appear in the order described here. This means that base layers are at the bottom, followed by overlaid polygons and lines, and finally markers appear at the top:

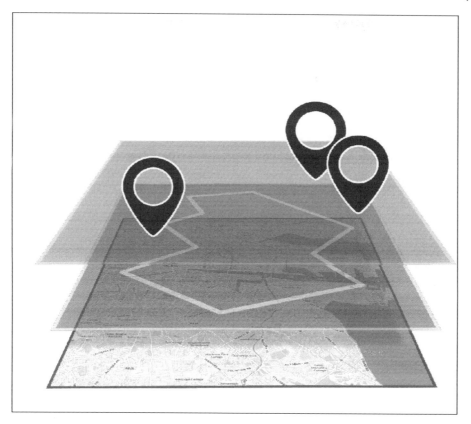

Using Mapbox.js, it is very easy to add as many layers as you want to display the data needed. We can create as many base layers as we want and switch freely between them.

In this recipe, we will do just this: we will create three different layers and switch between them. We will not use the other two types of layers, overlays and markers (we will do this in a while), but we will create multiple base layers and switch between them.

Switching between layers

We will continue using a starter project similar to the one created in the previous recipe. The starter project includes a base map layer and three buttons in the upper-right corner of the screen that allow us to switch between the other two types of layers.

We will create a function that will allow us to check whether a layer is already added; if not, it will add the layer on the screen. Perform the following steps:

1. Open the `chapter-4-example3-starter` project in your favorite text editor.

2. Jump into the `main.js` file. We will add a method to switch between the layers.

   Outside the scope of `window.onload()`, create a new JavaScript function called `switchLayer(map, layer)`. In this function, we will pass the `map` variable and the layer we want to add to the map, as follows:

   ```
   function switchLayer(map, layer) {
     if (map.hasLayer(layer)) {
       map.removeLayer(layer);
     }
     map.addLayer(layer);
   }
   ```

   In this function, we used two new methods of the Mapbox.js API. The first one is `hasLayer(<ILayer> layer)`, and it simply checks whether the map already contains that layer and returns `true` if this is the case.

   The other one is `removeLayer(<ILayer> layer)`. We do not want to indefinitely add layers to the map. In case a layer is already there, we first have to remove it. This method simply accepts a `layer` object to remove.

3. Within the `window.onload()` context, note that we already added the base layer to the map using `map.addLayer(baseLayer);`.

   As in the previous recipe, let's create an `onClick()` handler to switch to this layer in case it is not on screen, as follows:

   ```
   map.getContainer().querySelector('#base')
     .onclick = function() {
     switchLayer(map, baseLayer);
   };
   ```

   We will use the `switchLayer(map, layer)` function we created previously and we will pass `baseLayer` to be added to `map`.

4. Let's repeat the same procedure for the other two layers. Execute the following code:

```
var highwaysLayer = L.mapbox.tileLayer
    ('mapboxrecipes.3327d9fa');

map.getContainer().querySelector('#highways')
    .onclick = function() {
    switchLayer(map, highwaysLayer);
};

var terrainLayer = L.mapbox.tileLayer
    ('mapboxrecipes.6576d705');

map.getContainer().querySelector('#terrain')
    .onclick = function() {
    switchLayer(map, terrainLayer);
};
```

We added a variable called the `highways` layer that holds `tileLayer` with the Map ID `mapboxrecipes.3327d9f`; then we added a handler to switch to this layer when the `#highways` div is clicked on.

The same procedure is repeated for the terrain layer.

5. Now open `index.html` in a web browser and try switching between the three layers:

Adding markers and popups

In this recipe, you will learn how to add markers with popups dynamically. We will enhance the previous recipe, which displays a map, and we will add a button that will open a popup in which we can type coordinates.

When we click on the **OK** button, a new marker will be created, and the map will zoom and pan to the location of this marker; if there are multiple markers, it will zoom to fit them all.

How to do it...

Perform the following steps:

1. Create a map and add a base layer.
2. Then add new markers to the map using `L.marker([latitude, longitude]).addTo(map);`.
3. Use `bindPopup('enter html content here')` to bind a popup to the marker.

Adding a basic marker with a popup

Here are the steps to be performed:

1. Open the `chapter-4-example4-starter` project folder in your favorite text editor. The project contains the map we used in other recipes with a **New Marker** button. When this button is clicked on, it will trigger a new method that will open a prompt to type the coordinates. Let's create this method now.

2. Outside the scope of `window.onload()`, create the following method:

   ```
   function openDialog(map, layer) {

     var coordinates = prompt("Coordinates:", "42.3710,
       -71.0387");
     addNewMarker(coordinates, layer, map);

   }
   ```

   This will simply create a new prompt with the default coordinates 42.3710, -71.0387. When the user clicks on the **OK** button, it will call the `addNewMarker(coordinates, layer, map)` function and pass the coordinates. Let's create this method next.

3. After `openDialog(map, layer)`, create the following method:

```
function addNewMarker(coordinates, layer, map) {

    var coordinatesArray = coordinates.split(',');
    var coords = L.latLng(coordinatesArray[0],
      coordinatesArray[1]);

    var htmlContent = '<b>Coordinates:</b> ' +
      coordinatesArray[0] + ', ' + coordinatesArray[1] +
      '</br>' + '<img src="http://lorempixel.com/170/150/">';

    var marker = L.marker(coords, {
      icon: L.mapbox.marker.icon({
        'marker-color': '#aa0000',
        'marker-symbol': 'triangle'
      })
    }).bindPopup(htmlContent);

    marker.addTo(layer);
    map.fitBounds(layer.getBounds());

}
```

Let's explain what's going on in the preceding code:

- In the `coordinatesArray` variable, we split the coordinates, which is actually a comma-separated string, into an array.
- We created a `coords` variable using `L.latLng` and by passing the coordinates as in the previous recipes.
- In the `htmlContent` variable, we created the content that will display the coordinates along with a placeholder image in the marker popup.
- Finally, we created the marker using `L.marker` and by setting the icon color to red (`#aa0000`) and using the Maki symbol for triangle. We then bound the `htmlContent` we created earlier using `bindPopup(htmlContent);`.
- We added the marker to `featureLayer` using `marker.addTo(layer)`.

In this recipe, we added our markers to `featureLayer`. Mapbox allows us to combine and organize feature layers as we want. We can use `L.mapbox.featureLayer.addTo(mapOrLayer)` to add feature layers to other feature layers, creating our own hierarchy.

> ❑ The last step is to pan and zoom the map to fit all the markers. We did this with `map.fitBounds(layer.getBounds());`.

4. Finally, open `index.html` in your favorite web browser and try adding a couple of markers:

Creating markers using the geocoder

In the previous section, you learned how to create markers with popups using Mapbox.js.

Let's expand the recipe so that instead of typing coordinates—which, by the way, is not very user-friendly—it will also accept addresses, areas, or cities. To do this, we will use the Mapbox.js geocoder. Perform the following steps:

1. Open `main.js` in your favorite text editor.

2. The first step is to improve the `openDialog(map, layer)` function to accept coordinates and addresses and handle each case. We can do this via the following code:

```
function openDialog(map, layer) {

  var coordinates = prompt("Coordinates:", "42.3710,
    -71.0387");
  var regEx = /^[-+]?([1-8]?\d(\.\d+)?|90(\.0+)?),\s*[-+]
    ?(180(\.0+)?|((1[0-7]\d)|([1-9]?\d))(\.\d+)?)$/;

  var isCoordinates = regEx.test(coordinates);
```

```
if (isCoordinates) {
  addNewMarker(coordinates, layer, map);
} else {
  geocode(coordinates, layer, map);
}
}
```

We added a new variable called `regEx` with a hugely complicated regular expression. If you are not familiar with the regular expressions syntax, do not fear! You don't need to understand it; just remember that we will use it to distinguish whether the text entered into the prompt is an address or coordinates. This happens directly below the `isCoordinates` variable. If the text is coordinates, we will call `addNewMarker(coordinates, layer, map)` as before.

If the text is an address, we will call the `geocode` method and pass the coordinates variable (which stores the address in this case), the layer, and the map.

3. Let's create this `geocode` function now. Run the following code:

```
function geocode(address, coordinates, map) {
  var geocoder = L.mapbox.geocoder('mapbox.places');
  geocoder.query(address, showMap);

}
```

Here we have created a new geocoder using `L.mapbox.geocoder('mapbox.places')`. Then we passed the address and a callback function, `showMap`.

4. Let's create the geocoder `showMap` function now, as follows:

```
function showMap(err, data) {

  if (data.latlng) {
    var coordinates = String(data.latlng);
    addNewMarker(coordinates, featureLayer, map);
  }

}
```

The function will return `data`, which is a structure that also contains the coordinates we need to create the marker or an error (`err`). We will handle this just in case something comes back from the geocoder.

In this case, we will call `addNewMarker(coordinates, featureLayer, map)` and pass the coordinates we got back from the geocoder.

5. That's all! You just learned how to create markers from coordinates and get back coordinates from an address using geocoding. Open `index.html` in your browser and try to type an address:

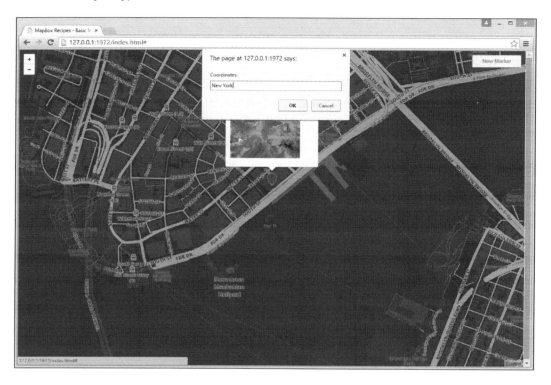

How it works...

We can create a new marker using `L.marker(<LatLng> latlng, <Marker options> options?)`. The essential parameter is `latlng`, which is a coordinate. In `<options>`, we can set up various parameters to customize the appearance of the marker. I will explain the most important ones here:

▶ `marker-symbol`: This allows us to select the symbol that will appear on top of the default marker icon. Note that this is not a custom icon. We will create one in the following recipe.

Symbols in Mapbox are provided in my Maki icon set. They are pixel-perfect icons especially created for web cartography. At `https://www.mapbox.com/maki/`, you can select a symbol, and it will show the string that needs to be passed in `marker-symbol` in order to make the preceding marker icon appear.

- ▶ `clickable`: This disables the mouse events on the marker.
- ▶ `title`: This shows text or HTML at the marker popup.
- ▶ `zIndexOffset`: This is the depth order that the marker will appear in. When a number passed in this parameter is higher than the numbers other markers have, it will appear at the front.

Clustering markers to improve our map

As we already saw, creating markers and adding them to a map is not a difficult task at all. There are circumstances in which creating the markers one by one may work; however, what happens if the data we want to visualize has thousands of records?

Populating the map with large amounts of data is *inefficient* performance-wise, and the lag dominates the user experience. The user will not be able to distinguish the markers and have a clear picture of what is going on in this crowded map. Surely, this is a poor user experience.

In this recipe, you will learn how to use **clustering** to present data in a more efficient and clean way.

How to do it...

Perform the following steps:

1. Import the **Leaflet.markercluster** plugin.
2. Create a new `featureLayer` and add the data you want to use as features.
3. Once the data in the `featureLayer` is loaded, create a `clusterGroup` and add the features layer to it.

Creating markers

Perform the following steps:

1. Open the `chapter-4-example6-starter` directory's `index.html` file in a browser. After a couple of seconds (depending on your Internet speed), several hundreds of markers will appear on the screen:

   This is how a large amount of data will be displayed without clustering. As you can understand, it's not practical at all, so let's fix this now.

2. Jump into the `index.html` file. We will need to link the markercluster plugin first. We will link the necessary JavaScript and CSS files.

   After the links to Mapbox.js and CSS files, but before our `main.js` link, we will insert the following code:

```
<script src='https://api.tiles.mapbox.com/mapbox.js/
  plugins/leaflet-markercluster/v0.4.0/
  leaflet.markercluster.js'></script>
<link href='https://api.tiles.mapbox.com/mapbox.js/
  plugins/leaflet-markercluster/v0.4.0/
  MarkerCluster.css' rel='stylesheet' />
<link href='https://api.tiles.mapbox.com/mapbox.js/
  plugins/leaflet-markercluster/v0.4.0/
  MarkerCluster.Default.css' rel='stylesheet' />
```

3. Jump into the `main.js` file. This time, we will not add the markers directly in our map, but we will use a GeoJSON file. We will use the response data from USGS to display the earthquakes occurring in the last month. After `map.addLayer(baseLayer)`, add the following code:

```
featureLayer = L.mapbox.featureLayer().loadURL
  ('http://earthquake.usgs.gov/earthquakes/
  feed/v1.0/summary/1.0_month.geojson');
```

We will use the `featureLayer.loadURL(url)` function to load the data of the GeoJSON file.

4. As `loadURL(url)` is an asynchronous function, we need to know when the GeoJSON is loaded to generate the clusters. We will use `on('ready', function(e)` to do this, as follows:

```
featureLayer.on('ready', function(e) {

});
```

5. Within the closures of the function, generate a new cluster group using `L.MarkerClusterGroup()`, as follows:

```
featureLayer.on('ready', function(e) {
  var clusterGroup = new L.MarkerClusterGroup();
});
```

6. Then, loop through the layers and add each one to `clusterGroup`. Finally, add the `clusterGroup` layer to the map. The complete function will be similar to the following:

```
featureLayer.on('ready', function(e) {

  var clusterGroup = new L.MarkerClusterGroup();

  e.target.eachLayer(function(layer) {
    clusterGroup.addLayer(layer);
  });

  map.addLayer(clusterGroup);

});
```

7. That's it! Open `index.html` into your browser and observe the results of clustering. Try to zoom in and out to see the clusters generated dynamically!

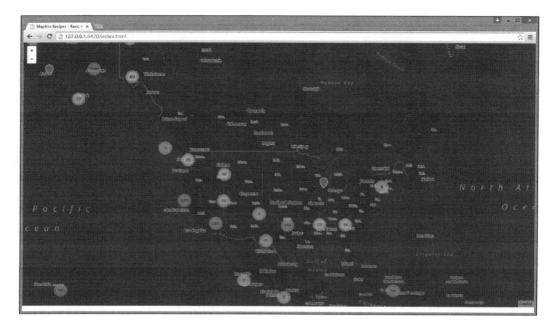

Creating a simple polyline and polygon

In this section, you will learn how to create polylines and polygons, and we will use two methods. The difference between the two is that polygons are closed, while polylines are open. An example of a use for polylines is to represent a path for driving directions; on the other hand, we can use polygons to represent a closed area, such as the bounds of a park.

The first method you need to learn is `L.polyline(<LatLng[]> latlngs, <Polyline options> options?)`. It takes an array of `<LatLng>` from the first point to the last. Each point will connect to the previous one.

You must have guessed that we will pass the color, weight, and other useful attributes of the polyline in <Polyline options>, right? If we inspect the documentation of <Polyline options>, we will notice that it accepts just two parameters, and none of them seems to do what we want. The trick is that L.Polyline extends the path, so <Polyline options> inherits from <path-options>. If we check the documentation for this, we will discover that it accepts color, weight, opacity, dashArray (if we are creating a dashed polyline), and other parameters that will help us to style the polyline.

Similarly, we will use L.polygon(<LatLng[]> latlngs, <Polyline options> options?) to draw a closed polygon. L.polygon inherits from L.polyline, and it will accept the same options, even though some of them make more sense used in a polygon, such as fill-color.

Perform the following steps:

1. Start by opening the starter project's chapter-4-example8-polylines-starter folder and going directly to the main.js file. As in the previous recipes, we will start with a simple full-screen map.

2. First, we will generate a <latlong> array to hold the coordinates for the polyline. Run the following:

```
var polylinePoints = [
    [42.366887, -71.058519],
    [42.364303, -71.063433],
    [42.362908, -71.063840],
    [42.361227, -71.063776],
    [42.361148, -71.069891]
];
```

3. Let's create the polyline options and hold them in a variable. It's easier to read the code this way, as follows:

```
var polylineOptions = {
  color: '#ff0000',
  weight: 12
};
```

4. It's time to create our polyline. We will pass polylinePoints and polylineOptions and add it to our map, as follows:

```
var polyline = L.polyline(polylinePoints,
    polylineOptions).addTo(map);
```

5. Finally, let's adjust the bounds to fit the polylines in our map:

```
var boundsOptions = {padding: [100,100]};
map.fitBounds(polyline.getBounds(), boundsOptions);
```

That's it! Let's take a look at what we created:

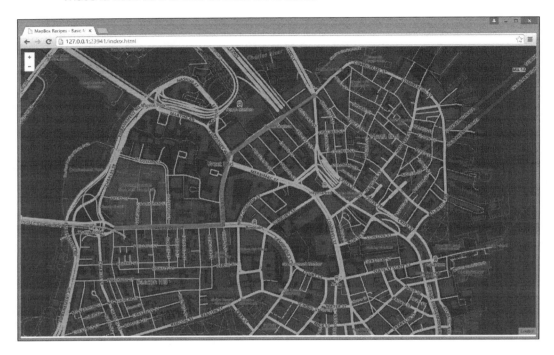

6. Great, the polyline is there! Now, let's add the polygon. We will follow the exact same steps. First, create some points and add them to a polygon variable, as follows:

```
var polygonPoints = [
    [42.363051, -71.059613],
    [42.362866, -71.058959],
    [42.362478, -71.058379],
    [42.361582, -71.057575],
    [42.362153, -71.056513],
    [42.362454, -71.057049],
    [42.362779, -71.057510],
    [42.363548, -71.058347],
    [42.363698, -71.058369],
    [42.363230, -71.059211]
];
```

7. Next, create `polygonOptions`. This time, we will set the color to green, as follows:

```
var polygonOptions = {
  color: '#00aa00',
  weight: 12
};
```

8. Finally, create `polygon` and add it to the map via the following lines:

```
var polygon = L.polygon(polygonPoints,
  polygonOptions).addTo(map);
```

Let's have a look at the final result:

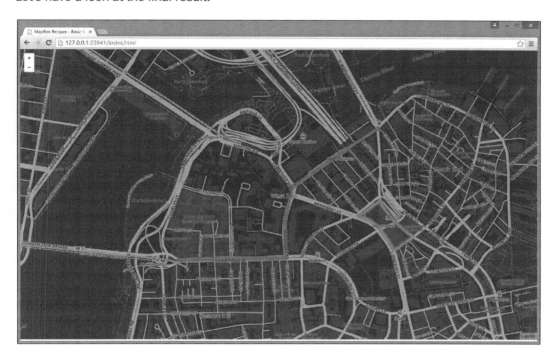

Getting mouse coordinates

One of the most important aspects of using maps is user interaction. Interacting with the map can be done in various ways, which also depends on the device used; for example, you can hover over a location using the mouse, but you can't do this using a touch-based device, such as a smartphone. In smartphones, you can use multitap or perform gestures, and these user interactions cannot be performed using the mouse.

In this recipe, you will learn how to use event listeners to trigger actions in order to implement user interaction in your map.

How to do it...

The condensed steps to be performed are as follows:

1. Create a map with `baseLayer`.

2. Then create an event listener using `map.on('mousemove', mouseMovedCallback)`.

3. In the callback method, get the latitude and longitude.

4. Now, construct an HTML file that shows the latitude and longitude and inject the HTML file into a div to display the mouse coordinates.

Let's perform these steps now:

1. Start by opening the starter project directory `chapter-4-example10-coordinates-starter` in your favorite text editor. The project contains a simple map with a base layer, `featuresLayer` (which will be used later), and a simple HTML `<div>` element with some CSS to hold our mouse coordinates.

2. Jump into `main.js`. After `featureLayer`, let's create a variable and get this div:

   ```
   var coordinatesBox = document.getElementById
       ('coordinates');
   ```

3. Now let's create the listener using the following code:

   ```
   map.on('mousemove', function(e) {
     coordinatesBox.innerHTML = e.latlng.toString();
   });
   ```

   We will register `mousemove` events and print the coordinates on the `<div>` element.

4. Add another listener to register click events, as follows:

   ```
   map.on('click', function(e) {
     coordinatesBox.innerHTML = "clicked: " + e.latlng.
       toString();
   });
   ```

5. Let's take a look at what we have:

We successfully subscribed to mousemove events, and the coordinates are printed inside the <div> element in the upper-left corner.

6. Let's create something more interesting than simply printing the coordinates. We will subscribe to a click event, and each time the user clicks, we will create a new marker, as follows:

```
map.on('click', function(e) {

  var marker = L.marker(e.latlng, {
    icon: L.mapbox.marker.icon({
      'marker-color': '#aa0000'
    })
  }).bindPopup(e.latlng.toString());

  marker.addTo(featureLayer);
  map.fitBounds(featureLayer.getBounds());

});
```

That's it!

Try clicking on the map. A new marker will be created each time you click, and the map will zoom to fit the bounds of `featureLayer`.

Clicking on a marker will display a popup with the coordinates, as shown in the following screenshot:

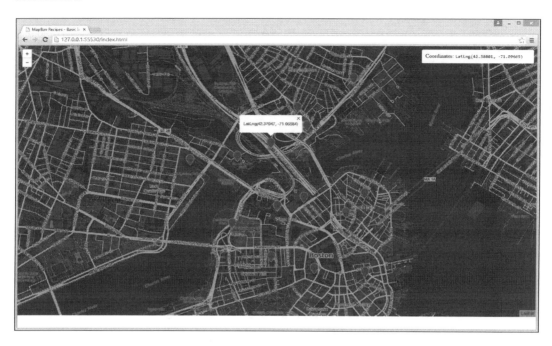

How it works...

We will use map events to get the mouse coordinates. You can listen to various types of events. Let's explore the most important ones, as follows:

- ► `click`: This refers to clicking the left mouse button or tapping on a mobile or touchscreen device
- ► `dblclick`: This refers to double-clicking the left mouse button or double tapping
- ► `mouseover`: This is triggered when the mouse enters the map
- ► `load`: This is triggered when the map is initialized
- ► `mousemove`: This is triggered when the mouse moves over a layer of the map
- ► `dragstart`: This is triggered when the user starts dragging a marker
- ► `drag`: This is triggered repeatedly as long as the user drags the marker
- ► `dragend`: This is triggered when the user stops dragging the marker

There are other types of events you can subscribe to that don't have to do with user interaction but are still extremely useful:

- ▶ add: This is triggered when a marker is added to the map
- ▶ remove: This is triggered when a marker is removed from the map
- ▶ popupopen: This is triggered when a popup of a marker is opened
- ▶ popupclose: This is triggered when a popup of a marker is closed

To subscribe to an event, you can simply use an event listener, such as addEventListener(<String> type, <Function> fn, <Object> context?).

Luckily, Leaflet has an alias which is simpler to use; take a look at the following:

```
map.on('click', function(e) {
  alert(e.latlng);
});
```

If you are planning to remove the listener at a later stage, you can instead use a function, as follows:

```
function onClickListener(e) {
  alert(e.latlng);
}

map.on('click', onClickListener);

map.off('click', onClickListener);
```

Working with controls

In this recipe, we will learn how to add controls to the map. Actually, our maps already use controls. The zoom control in the upper-left corner and the attribution in the lower-right corner are examples of controls.

How to do it...

We need to do the following:

1. Create a control and customize it by passing the options.
2. Add the control to the map.

Adding a zoom control to the map

Perform the following steps:

1. Open the `chapter-4-example-13-controls` folder in your favorite text editor. The project is already configured and has a base layer.

2. In `main.js`, let's modify the map to disable the default controls via the following code:

```
var map = L.map('map', {
  zoomControl: false,
  attributionControl: false
}).setView(latlong, 15);
```

This will disable the zoom and attribution controls. We will then add our own.

3. Let's add the zoom control first. Execute the following code:

```
var zoomControl = L.control.zoom({position: 'topright',
  zoomInTitle: 'Click to zoom in', zoomOutTitle: 'Click
  to zoom out'});
zoomControl.addTo(map);
```

In the control options, we set the `position` to `topright` and also set a custom `zoomInTitle` and `zoomOutTitle`.

4. Next, we will customize the attribution control via the following script:

```
var attributionControl = L.control.attribution
  ({position: 'bottomleft', prefix: '(c) 2015, MapBox
  Recipes'});
attributionControl.addTo(map);
```

In this case, we simply passed plain text in the `prefix` parameter, but you are free to pass HTML if you want.

5. Finally, we will add the `L.control.layers(<Layer Config> baseLayers?, <Layer Config> overlays?, <Control.Layers options> options?)` control. It accepts both base layers and overlaid layers in the parameters. Before using it, we need to make some modifications to our project.

6. First, let's add two more layers to our project. After the `mapboxTiles` variable, add `highwaysLayer` and `terrainLayer`, as follows:

```
var highwaysLayer = L.mapbox.tileLayer
    ('mapboxrecipes.3327d9fa');
var terrainLayer = L.mapbox.tileLayer
    ('mapboxrecipes.6576d705');
```

7. Next, instead of adding a single layer to the map, we have the option to pass an array of layers when creating the `map` variable. We can use the following code for this:

```
var map = L.map('map', {
    zoomControl: false,
    attributionControl: false,
    layers:[terrainLayer, highwaysLayer, mapboxTiles]
}).setView(latlong, 15);
```

8. Make sure you delete the following lines because we have already passed `baseLayer` in the preceding array:

```
var baseLayer = L.mapbox.tileLayer
    ('mapboxrecipes.kk6jp52i');
map.addLayer(baseLayer);
```

9. Next, we will create an object to hold our layers, as follows:

```
var baseLayers = {
    "Terrain Layer": terrainLayer,
    "Highways Layer": highwaysLayer,
    "Base Layer": mapboxTiles
};
```

The string is just the text we will show in the layers control.

10. Add the layers control to the map and pass the object we just created:

```
L.control.layers(baseLayers).addTo(map);
```

That's it! In the *Working with base layers* recipe, we already discussed a way to add and remove layers to the map. We used more traditional methods to do this, but now you have also learned that we can provide the same functionality using Mapbox controls.

Open `index.html` in your browser and try switching between the layers:

How it works...

`Control` is the base class of all controls. It optionally accepts `<Control options>` `options?`. We can set the `position` property to specify where the control will appear on the screen.

The Mapbox.js API has several different types of controls. Let's explore the most common ones:

- `L.control.zoom(<Control.Zoom options> options?)`: This is the zoom control we already know. You can customize it further by setting the `position` value and what text it will show in the buttons.

- `L.control.attribution(<Control.Attribution options> options?)`: This is the attribution control. In case you need to add an attribution to the map, you can pass the HTML file in the `prefix` parameter.

- `L.control.layers(<Layer Config> baseLayers?, <Layer Config> overlays?, <Control.Layers options> options?)`: This is a control we haven't seen before. It allows us to switch between the base and overlaid layers.

Adding interactivity to your map with UTFGrid

In this recipe, we will create an interactive map using **UTFGrid**. The benefit of using UTFGrid instead of markers is that UTFGrids can handle a lot more data than it is possible to handle otherwise.

If your map needs to interact with several thousands of bits of data, it is no longer viable to fetch this data in a single pass, then cache it in the browser, and generate markers from it. It's inefficient performance-wise, but luckily, UTFGrid comes to the rescue in such extreme cases.

How to do it...

The steps to be performed are as follows:

1. Create a map with TileMill. Use the templates section of TileMill to add interactivity to the map.

2. Upload the map to Mapbox (or host it in your own server).

3. Create `L.mapbox.gridLayer` and pass the Map ID.

4. Then use the `map.on('click', onClickCallback)` handler to generate a popup when a user clicks on a `gridLayer`.

Creating an interactive map using TileMill

Fire up TileMill. We will use it to create our interactive map. Perform the following steps:

1. Create a new project and give it a name.

2. Keep the default `#countries` layer with the default styling. We will not use the style of this layer anyway, just the UTF data that we will embed in the tiles.

3. In the `chapter-4-example10-utf-shape` folder in the accompanying code bundle, there is a shapefile containing the counties in the United States (this folder is also hosted at `https://bitbucket.org/billkastanakis/mapbox-cookbook/src`). Custom shapefiles can be created using QGIS or other GIS software, or they can be downloaded from organizations and other service providers. You can open the shapefile in QGIS to explore the data in it, as shown in the following screenshot:

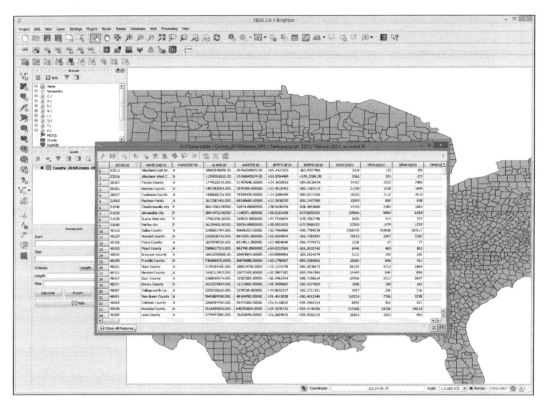

4. Let's import it into TileMill. Go to the **Layers** palette and click on the **Add Layer** button.

5. Give the new layer an ID (I named mine #counties) and select **County_2010Census_DP1.shp** as the data source from the folder.

6. Click on **Save**.

7. Let's give the new layer some basic styling just to see where it's located via the following code:

```
#counties {
   line-color: #e2e2e2;
     line-width: 2;
       polygon-fill: #006600;
}
```

8. Don't forget that we need to save after we finish typing the CartoCSS code to see the changes on the live map.

9. Now let's add the interactivity. Click on the hand icon to open the **Templates** screen and click on the **Teaser** tab. At the bottom of the screen, select the counties layer as the interaction data layer.

10. The moment you select the interaction layer, the text field below it will be populated with values containing the attribute names inside the so-called moustache tags!

 You can find out more about the **moustache** templating language at the official GitHub site at http://mustache.github.io/.

11. You can define the content you want to display for hover (or first tap on a mobile) in the main text editor. The following section is just basic HTML with some inline CSS to style the fixed width and height popup box. In the box, we will simply display the county name that exists in the {{{NAMELSAD10}}} field:

```
<div style="text-align:center; width: 220px; height: 70px;
   font-size: 18px;">

   <strong>{{{NAMELSAD10}}}</strong><br>

</div>
```

This is shown in the following screenshot:

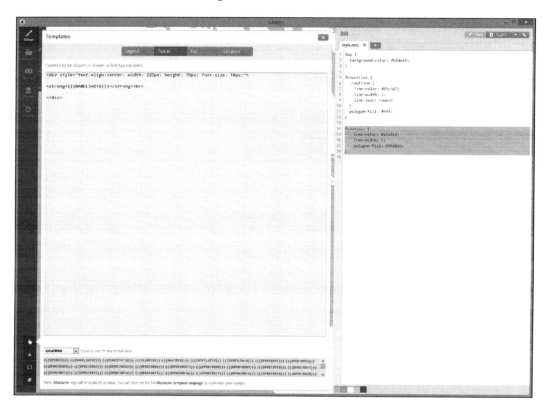

12. Go back to the main TileMill screen and try letting the mouse hover over US. You will see that the county is now displayed in the upper-right corner:

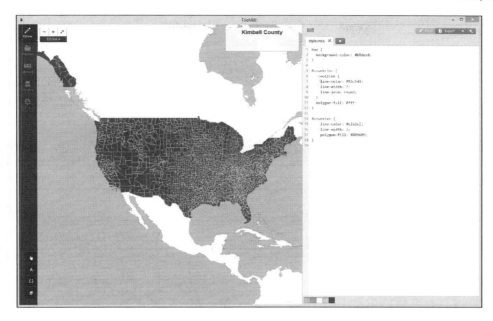

13. The last step is to export the tiles and host them on the Mapbox servers. TileMill can do both in one step. Click on **Export** in the upper-right corner and select **MBTiles** from the export options. Don't forget to limit the zoom and region to manageable levels, as you learned in the TileMill recipes in *Chapter 3, TileMill and Mapbox Studio*. Set the center also somewhere in the United States:

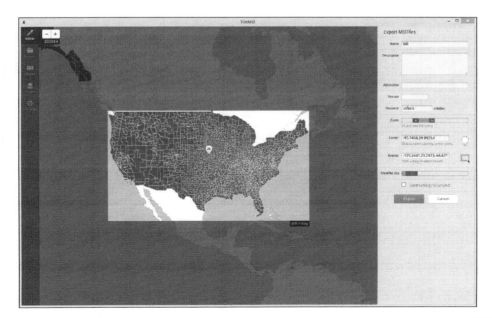

Creating an interactive map using Mapbox.js

Now that we have the tiles exported and uploaded to Mapbox, let's take a look at how we can use Mapbox.js to fetch the data embedded in the tiles using UTFGrid:

1. Open the `chapter-4-example10-utf-starter` folder in your text editor. As usual, the project contains a base layer added using Mapbox.js.

2. In the `main.js` file, let's create our UTFGrid layer. After `map.addLayer(baseLayer)`, add the following lines:

   ```
   var gridLayer = L.mapbox.gridLayer
       ('mapboxrecipes.utftest');
   map.addLayer(gridLayer);
   ```

   `L.mapbox.gridLayer` loads the UTFGrid tiles from the `mapboxrecipes.utftest` Map ID and adds them to our map.

3. To access the interactive parts of the map, we need to use `L.mapbox.gridControl(layer, options)`. Let's add this now as follows:

   ```
   var myGridControl = L.mapbox.gridControl
       (gridLayer).addTo(map);
   ```

4. Finally, let's create a popup for when a user clicks on a county by executing the following code:

   ```
   gridLayer.on('click', function(e) {
       if (!e.data) return;
       var popup = L.popup().setLatLng(e.latLng).
           setContent(e.data.NAMELSAD10).openOn(map);
   });
   ```

That's it! We have now used Mapbox.js to fetch UTFGrid data from an interactive layer that we created in TileMill. Using this powerful technique, we can have thousands of bits of data available without significant overhead. Open `index.html` in your browser to take a look at the result:

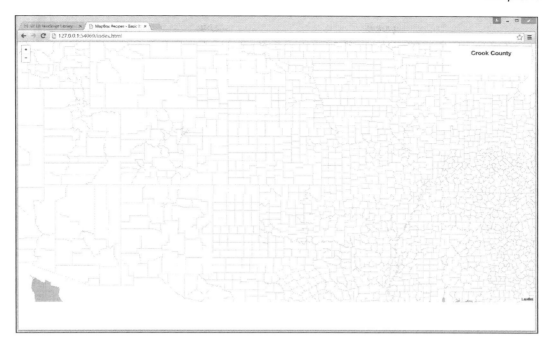

How it works...

UTFGrid actually stores data in the tiles. The tiles currently displayed on the screen at this specific region and zoom level have the data embedded in them.

There are rare cases in which a user needs to interact with data that is not displayed on the screen. In these cases, this specific recipe does not work because those tiles are never loaded.

Creating a choropleth map

In this recipe, we will create a **choropleth** map. In this type of map, the shaded areas represent the measurement of a variable—for example, population density, total population, or temperature. Higher values in the variable are represented by a denser color.

We will now create a choropleth map that shows the education level in the United States.

How to do it...

The condensed steps are as follows:

1. Generate a map with a base layer.
2. Generate a GeoJSON that contains the data we want to display, as well as a polygon of the area that the data represents.
3. Create a GeoJSON layer using `L.geoJson`. Enumerate through the data, and for each feature, use `style(<GeoJSON> featureData)` to style the polygon.

Let's perform these steps now:

1. Start by opening the `chapter-4-example11-choropleth-starter` project in your favorite text editor. There is already a configured base map, as in the previous recipes. Open the `index.html` file.
2. We will import a `states.js` file using the following line:

   ```
   <script src='data/states.js'></script>
   ```

   It's a GeoJSON file that contains the states' polygon data along with the state name and the education level, as seen in the following example:

   ```
   var data = {"type":"FeatureCollection","features":[
     {"type":"Feature","id":"01","properties":
     {"name":"Alabama","hs":82.1,"bd":22.0,"ad":7.7},
     "geometry":{"type":"Polygon","coordinates":
     [[[-87.359296,35.00118],[-85.606675,34.984749],
     [-85.431413,34.124869]….
   ]]}},
   ```

3. Open the `main.js` file. Let's create some classes that will help us with our task. The first one is a function that will just return a hex color when passing a value, as follows:

```
function returnColor(value) {

    if (value > 90) return '#081d58';
    else if (value > 90) return '#253494';
    else if (value > 88) return '#225ea8';
    else if (value > 85) return '#1d91c0';
    else if (value > 83) return '#41b6c4';
    else if (value > 82) return '#7fcdbb';
    else if (value > 81) return '#c7e9b4';
    else if (value > 80) return '#edf8b1';
    else if (value < 80) return '#ffffd9';

}
```

 Color Brewer is a great website that will help you choose a color scheme. Visit `http://colorbrewer2.org/` to design you own color scheme!

4. The next function will generate a style for the states. It will use our previous function to pick the color based on the `feature.properties.hs` value:

```
function style(feature) {

    return {
        weight: 2,
        opacity: 0.6,
        dashArray: '6',
        fillColor: returnColor(feature.properties.hs),
        color: 'white',
        fillOpacity: 0.75
    };

}
```

5. We are now ready to style the states. Within the `onload` function, enumerate through the GeoJSON data and generate a style for each state based on the `feature.properties.hs` value, as follows:

```
geojson = L.geoJson(data, {
    style: style
}).addTo(map);
```

6. We are ready to preview our choropleth map. Open the `index.html` file in your web browser:

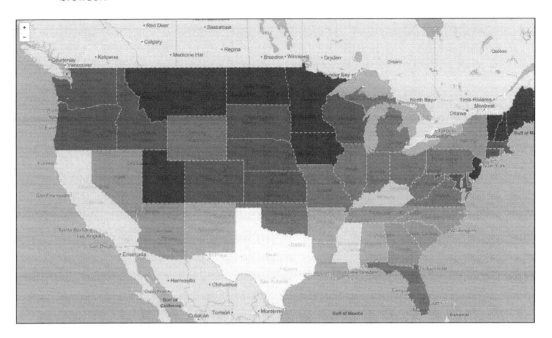

Great! With a few simple steps, we already have a great map, but these colors mean nothing at the moment. Let's add a legend.

7. Create a new function that will include the code to generate the legend, as follows:

```
function generateLegend() {

    var legend = L.control({position: 'bottomright'});

    legend.onAdd = function (map) {

        var div = L.DomUtil.create('div', 'info legend'),
            grades = [90, 88, 85, 83, 82, 81, 79];

        div.innerHTML  = '<i style="background:' +
returnColor(grades[0])  + '"></i>> 90<br>' +
                        '<i style="background:' +
returnColor(grades[1])  + '"></i>88-90<br>' +
                        '<i style="background:' +
returnColor(grades[2])  + '"></i>85-88<br>' +
```

```
                      '<i style="background:' +
returnColor(grades[3])   + '"></i>83-85<br>' +
                      '<i style="background:' +
returnColor(grades[4])   + '"></i>81-83<br>' +
                      '<i style="background:' +
returnColor(grades[5])   + '"></i>80-81<br>' +
                      '<i style="background:' +
returnColor(grades[6])   + '"></i>< 80<br>';
        return div;

    }

    return legend;
}
```

8. In `onload()`, call the function and add the legend to the map, as shown in the following code:

```
var legend = generateLegend().addTo(map);
```

Have a look at the map now:

9. Great, we now have a legend! However, it is still missing interaction. It will be great if our visitors can hover over the states to view the education level details.

So, let's do this now. First of all, we will create three new functions that will be triggered by our listeners on the `mouseover`, `mouseout`, and `click` events via the following code:

```
function highlight(e) {

  var layer = e.target;

  layer.setStyle({
    color: '#fff',
    fillOpacity: 0.85,
    weight: 5
  });

  info.update(layer.feature.properties);

}

function reset(e) {

  geojson.resetStyle(e.target);
  info.update();

}

function zoomToFeature(e) {
    map.fitBounds(e.target.getBounds());
}
```

10. In the `highlight` function, we will set a thick outline, the `reset` function will reset the style, and `zoomToFeature` will fit the map to the state bounds. Add a function with listeners as follows:

```
function onEachFeature(feature, layer) {
  layer.on({
    mouseover: highlight,
    mouseout: reset,
    click: zoomToFeature
  });
}
```

11. Don't forget to add the listeners to each state by modifying GeoJSON; use the following code for this:

```
geojson = L.geoJson(data, {
  style: style,
  onEachFeature: onEachFeature
}).addTo(map);
```

12. If you preview the project now, you will be able to see the highlight effect when you let the cursor hover over the states. The final step is to execute the following code to show an information box with the education level. We already have a div for this in the index.html file:

```
<div id="info"></div>
```

The div has some basic CSS styling, as can be seen in the following script:

```
#info {
    padding: 6px 8px;
    font: 14px/16px Arial, Helvetica, sans-serif;
    background: white;
    box-shadow: 0 0 15px rgba(0,0,0,0.2);
    border-radius: 5px;
}

#info h4 {
    margin: 0 0 5px;
    color: #777;
}
```

13. In the onload function, it's time to add a control that will generate the content displayed in the information box, as follows:

```
info = L.control();

info.onAdd = function(map) {
  this.infoDiv = document.getElementById('info');
  this.update();
  return this.infoDiv;
};

info.update = function (stateData) {
    this.infoDiv.innerHTML = '<h4>US Education Level</h4>' +
(stateData ?
            '<b>' + stateData.name + '</b><br />'
              + stateData.hs + '% High School</br>'
              + stateData.bd + '% College</br>'
```

```
                          + stateData.ad + '% University</br>'
              : 'Hover to show education level');
      };

      info.addTo(map);
```

14. Finally, modify the `highlight(e)` and `reset(e)` listeners to update the information box via the following code:

```
function highlight(e) {
  ….
  info.update(layer.feature.properties);
}

function reset(e) {
  geojson.resetStyle(e.target);
  info.update();
}
```

That's it! Open the `index.html` file and enjoy your choropleth map!

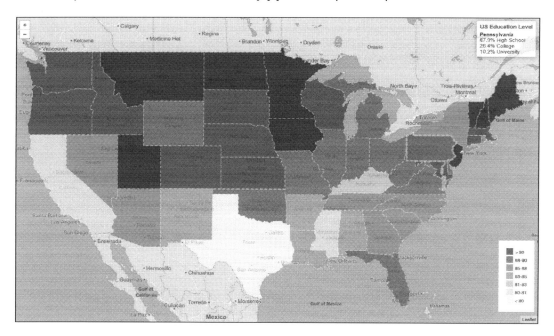

How it works...

The GeoJSON layer loads a file that contains the polygon data for the states, as well as the state name and the percentage of those educated to high school, college, and university level. To load the GeoJSON, we will use the following line:

```
L.geoJson(<Object> geojson?, <GeoJSON options> options?)
```

`L.geoJson` optionally accepts a GeoJSON object. We will pass the data we already have. The method will parse the GeoJSON data and generate feature layers.

On creation, we will use `style(<GeoJSON> featureData)` to style the polygon. Then, for each created feature layer, we will call `onEachFeature(<GeoJSON> featureData, <ILayer> layer)` to add interactivity to the map.

Each time the mouse hovers over a state, we will highlight it, and on mouseout, we will reset the style. A double-click handler can be added to zoom in to the state when the user performs this action.

Creating a heat map

In this recipe, we will create a heat map. A heat map usually visualizes the data range using a *pseudo color*, with the hotter colors being the higher values and the colder colors representing the lower range values.

How to do it...

The plugin we will use requires the data to be in a specific format, which is an array of *[latitude, longitude, altitude]*. It's unlikely that data in this format will be available from services, so first of all, the task is to enumerate through the actual data and format it as required.

Next, we have to create `heatLayer`, which is provided by the **Leaflet.heat** plugin, pass the data and options, and add it to the map. We will perform the following steps in this recipe:

1. Start by opening the `chapter-4-example12- heat-starter` project and opening the `index.html` file. We need to import the `leaflet-heat` plugin, so add the following line after the Mapbox.js scripts:

   ```
   <script src='https://api.tiles.mapbox.com/
     mapbox.js/plugins/leaflet-heat/v0.1.3/
     leaflet-heat.js'></script>
   ```

2. We also need to import our data. Normally, you will fetch the data from an API or other sources, but in this case, let's keep it simple and just import it using the following line:

```
<script src='js/earthquakes.js'></script>
```

The data comes from the USGS Earthquakes API. Here is an example request to fetch earthquakes of magnitude 5 or larger for a date range:

```
http://earthquake.usgs.gov/fdsnws/event/1/query?format=geojson&sta
rttime=2015-04-26&minmagnitude=5
```

This is shown in the following screenshot:

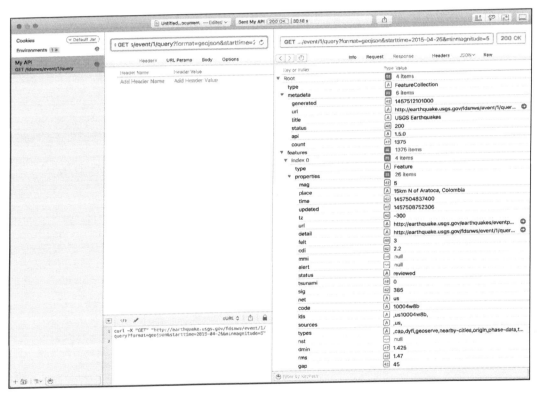

3. Now, open the `main.js` file. We need to enumerate through the data and generate objects that Leaflet.heat would understand. Ideally, in this case, if the API were ours, it would probably return the data format as required to avoid double processing in large datasets.

Each object will have a longitude, latitude, and an altitude value:

```
var data = Array();

earthquakes.features.forEach(function(feature) {

   var heatData = [feature.geometry.coordinates[0],
      feature.geometry.coordinates[1],
      feature.properties.mag];
   data.push(heatData);

});
```

4. Finally, we will use Leaflet.heat and pass the data array we just created. The plugin is available at GitHub at `https://github.com/Leaflet/Leaflet.heat`.

It accepts various parameters, allowing you to customize the appearance of the heat map even further. Let's consider some of the available options:

- `minOpacity`: This allows you to set the minimum opacity of the heat
- `max`: This is the maximum point of intensity
- `radius`: This is the radius of each point on the heat map
- `gradient`: This allows us to set a custom color gradient for the heat map

Add the following line of code after we parse our data:

```
var heat = L.heatLayer(data, {radius: 25, max: 0.01}).
   addTo(map);
```

We set the `max: 001` value to make the heat map more intense.

5. That's it! Open the `index.html` in your web browser to see the result, as shown in the following screenshot:

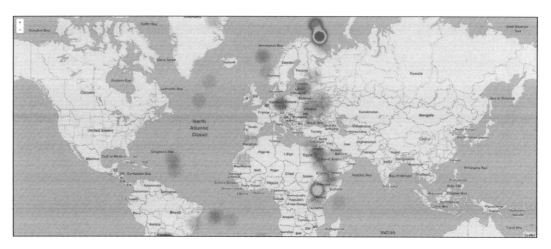

How it works...

Leaflet is known for its very active community and great variety of plugins. We used a plugin called Leaflet.heat to help us create the heat map. The plugin actually generates colored semi-transparent markers and intelligently blends them, creating the illusion of a heat map.

Mapbox.js Advanced

5

In this chapter, we will cover the following recipes:

- ▸ Adding external data to your map
- ▸ Adding a time dimension to your map
- ▸ Comparing two maps at the same time
- ▸ Adding a WMS layer from GeoServer to your map
- ▸ Adding ArcGIS layers from a server or from online
- ▸ Adding Fusion Tables to your map
- ▸ Adding Foursquare data to your map

Introduction

In this chapter, we will continue our exploration of Mapbox.js by using more advanced examples and several different third-party plugins that will help us integrate with external services and APIs.

Adding external data to your map

Leaflet (which Mapbox.js is based on) only supports the GeoJSON format out of the box. What if we want to add other types of data to our maps? As we saw in the previous chapter, Leaflet has an incredibly strong community that creates plugins. The plugin we are going to use, and which is going to help us accomplish this task, is called **Omnivore**. Omnivore is capable of loading several different file formats. We briefly discussed some of them in previous recipes:

▶ **Well-known text** (**WKT**): This is a text markup language for representing vector geometry. It supports points, lines, polygons, multipolygons, curves, surfaces, and many other types of vector geometry. There is a binary equivalent of this format called **WKB**.

▶ **Keyhole Markup Language** (**KML**): This is an XML-based format used to display geographic data. It is mostly used by Google.

▶ **GPX exchange format**: This is an XML-based format that is mostly used to describe waypoints, tracks, and routes. Most of the GPS found on the market can export in this file format. The Google Directions API also returns GPX data.

▶ **Comma-separated values** (**CSV**): This is a common format that stores tabular data in plain text form. Most of the applications on the market can export in this format.

▶ **TopoJSON**: This is an extension of the GeoJSON format that also encodes topology.

There are formats that are not mentioned in the preceding list, not because they are not important, but mostly because we will need to use the whole book to cover them all. Mapbox and Leaflet are great and extensive platforms, with plugins to load almost anything you'll ever need. One of the formats worth mentioning is **GML**.

How to do it...

1. Link Omnivore to your project.

2. Use `omnivore.kml(url)` or `omnivore.gpx(url)` to get a Leaflet layer back from files.

3. Add the returned layer to your map.

4. Optionally, use event listeners such as `.on('ready', function() {})` to handle additional code when the file is loaded.

Loading external data

Perform the following steps:

1. Open the `chapter 5 - importing` folder from the code files in your favorite text editor. Head directly to the `index.html` file. The first thing that we need to do is link the Omnivore plugin. Add the following line just before `<script src='js/main.js'></script>`:

   ```
   <script src='https://api.tiles.mapbox.com/
     mapbox.js/plugins/leaflet-omnivore/v0.2.0/
     leaflet-omnivore.min.js'></script>
   ```

2. The project is already set up to include a Mapbox base map. Let's load a KML file using Omnivore. It's easier to create a separate function:

   ```
   function loadKML(map) {
     var kmlSample = omnivore.kml('/kml/KML_Samples.kml')
     .on('ready', function() {
       map.fitBounds(kmlSample.getBounds());
     }).addTo(map);
   }
   ```

   We simply use `omnivore.kml(url)` to load and parse a KML file. This method will return a layer, so we can add that layer directly to our map.

Warning

Omnivore uses an AJAX request to get the file and parse it. The file must be in the same domain with the project, otherwise it will require **CORS** (**Cross-Origin Resource Sharing**) support for the server where the file is hosted and for the user's browser. CORS is a mechanism that allows resource files such as JavaScript and fonts to be shared between domains.

   We also have the event handler `'ready'` to make sure that the KML data is fully loaded before we use `.fitBounds` to fit the KML to our map.

You can also use the `.on('error', function() {})` event handler to handle errors in case Omnivore can't load or parse the data.

3. Make sure you call the function inside the `onLoad()` scope, just after `var map = L.map('map').addLayer(mapboxTiles).setView(latlong, 15);`:

   ```
   loadKML(map);
   ```

   Believe it or not, that's all that is needed to load an external KML file to Mapbox. It's incredibly simple and powerful.

4.   Make sure you save `main.js`, and open `index.html` in your web browser:

Loading a GPX file

We are going to use the same methodology to load a GPX file using Omnivore. Perform these steps:

1.   Let's continue from where we left in the previous section. Open the `main.js` file and create a new function with the following code:

```
function loadGPX(map) {

  var customLayer = L.geoJson(null, {
    style: function(feature) {
      console.log(feature);
      return { color: "#cc0000",  weight: 5, opacity: 0.95
        };
    }
  });

  var gpxSample = omnivore.gpx('/gpx/BogusBasin.gpx', null,
    customLayer)
  .on('ready', function() {
    map.fitBounds(gpxSample.getBounds());
  })
```

```
        .addTo(map);
}
```

In this case, we will create a GeoJSON `customLayer` to style the Omnivore GPX file, which we will load next.

To load the GPX file, follow almost the same steps as in the previous recipe. You can still use `var gpxSample = omnivore.gpx('/gpx/BogusBasin.gpx')` without passing the null and custom layer that we added, and the GPX will load just fine.

2. Replace `loadKML(map)` in `onLoad` with `loadGPX(map)`.

3. Save and open `index.html` in your browser:

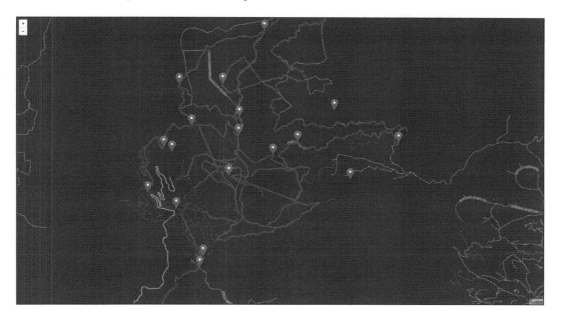

This is the end of the recipe. As you can see, Omnivore makes importing and styling various formats really simple.

> To load CSV, TopoJSON, and WPK files, use the following functions:
> - `omnivore.wkt('a.wkt').addTo(map);`
> - `omnivore.csv('a.csv').addTo(map);`
> - `omnivore.topojson('a.topojson').addTo(map);`

How it works...

Omnivore parses the supported formats internally, using parsers that are already well tested. It uses `https://github.com/mapbox/wellknown` to parse WKT, `https://github.com/mapbox/csv2geojson` to parse CSV, `https://github.com/mapbox/togeojson` to parse GPX and KML, and `https://github.com/mbostock/topojson` to parse TopoJSON files.

Omnivore is actually called a *bridge* plugin since it actually acts as a bridge between plugins that are already available separately.

Adding a time dimension to your map

In this recipe, we will learn how to visualize data over time. For that purpose, we will use **CartoDB** and a plugin called **Torque**. As an example, we are going to plot the paths of airplanes as they depart from Miami International Airport.

How to do it...

The following steps need to be performed:

1. First of all, we need to transform the data that we want to import into CartoDB to a format that is easy for the import tool to convert.
2. Click on your dataset and import your data into CartoDB.
3. Make sure that the imported data has a timestamp field and that it is correctly georeferenced.
4. Link Torque to your project.
5. Create a Torque CartoCSS style to stylize the markers generated by the plugin.
6. Create a new `torqueLayer` and make sure that you pass the style, user account, and the table.

Torque is the Leaflet plugin we are going to use in order to plot our data over time. Imagine Torque data as a cube with the front side as a two-dimensional map, and the Z direction as the time.

The way Torque works is that it fetches the data from the CartoDB database. It then looks for the georeferenced fields defined in CartoDB to get the locations of the markers. The last step is drawing the markers based on the date field defined in our dataset. The map behind Torque markers can be any Mapbox map, including overlaid maps, with or without feature layers.

To style the markers, Torque uses a subset of CartoCSS with custom Torque-specific properties. Apart from the usual size and color values, it also uses compositing blending modes in order to style the final result over the maps. The results can be drawn using the **commutative** mode, which plots the data over time *without removing the previous data from the map*. Optionally, we can also turn off the **cumulative** mode and simply draw each frame, clearing out the markers before the next frame is drawn.

To further customize the style, Torque allows us to define the style of the previous frames independently, giving us the option to have unlimited styling options.

Importing the data to CartoDB

Perform the following steps:

1. First of all, we need to sign up and create an account with CartoDB. Head to `https://cartodb.com/` and click on **SIGN UP**. You don't need a credit card to have an account at CartoDB. They offer a free plan with a limit of 50 MB, as well as a trial if you need more. Both will serve us just fine for the scope of this recipe.

2. Log in, click on the **Maps** combo box next to your account name in the upper-left corner of the screen, and select **Your datasets**.

3. Here you will see a list of the datasets that you have created already. Click on **NEW DATASET** and you will be presented with an import screen.

    You can import CSV, XLS, ZIP, MML, GPX, SHP, ODS, and other data files as well as open files directly from Google Drive, Dropbox, or even MailChip!

    I have already prepared a dataset for this recipe. It contains the flight data for departures from Miami International Airport (ICAO: KMIA, 25.793333, -80.290556).

    To generate the data, I have used a flight-tracking API called **FlightStats**. Other services, such as **FlightAware** and **FlightRadar24**, also have an API for tracking flights.

    Since we are going to import the data into CartoDB, *they need to be formatted in a specific way*, and should be as simple as possible. Very complex files often don't import correctly.

    For this recipe, I am using a simple JSON file that contains an array of flights. Each flight has the latitude, longitude, and timestamp fields, as well as the callsign, flight ID, speed, and altitude fields which are not used here.

    The latitude, longitude, and date fields are required in order to visualize the positions of flights over time; without these three fields, this would not be possible.

4. It's now time to import the data. Select **Data file** and browse to the `50flightspermin.json` file contained in the `chapter5 - torque` folder. Once you have selected the file, click on **CONNECT DATASET**.

CartoDB will process the file, and you will be presented with a table of the data that you have just imported.

5. From here, we can perform several operations if required. Let's rename the table first. Click on **table_50flightspermin** displayed in the top-left corner of the screen, and rename it `flights`.

6. Next we need to georeference (associate a data type with the location) the data. To do that, click on the **Edit** combo box in the top-right corner and select **Georeference**. Select the **latitude** and **longitude** column of the data table, and click on **CONTINUE**.

CartoDB offers several different ways to georeference data. You can use city names, postal codes, addresses, and even IP addresses!

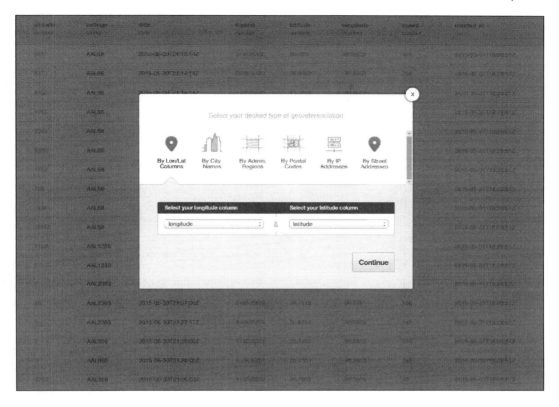

7. Make sure that the date column is date type data. A string date will not work with Torque. Most of the time, CartoDB can convert string data types to dates if you click on the **date** column combo box, select **Change data type**, and then click on **date**.

In case CartoDB is unable to convert your string date to date type data, there is another way to accomplish the task. You can use PostgreSQL queries to manipulate the data. On the right sidebar, there is an **SQL** button. Click on that, and write a query for modifying the date column string data to an ISO 8601 date format. The following steps give an example query. First, create a new column to store the new date:

```
ALTER TABLE flights ADD newdate TIMESTAMP;
```

Then convert the date:

```
UPDATE flights SET newdate = to_timestamp(olddate, 'MM/
DD/YY HH24:MI')
```

Modify `'MM/DD/YYHH24:MM'` to the format used in the old date field.

8. Once you have modified the table and the date, click on **MAP VIEW** to visualize the data:

If the georeferencing worked correctly, you will be able to view the data on the map. Our data is now ready to be used in Torque.

Using torque to visualize data over time

Perform the following steps:

1. Open the `chapter 5 - torque` folder in your favorite text editor. The project contains a preconfigured standard base layer map, as usual.

2. Append the following code after `var map = L.map...`:

```
var style =
'Map {' +
'-torque-time-attribute: "date";' +
'-torque-aggregation-function: "count(cartodb_id)";' +
'-torque-frame-count: 760;' +
'-torque-animation-duration: 5;' +
'-torque-resolution: 2' +
'}' +
'#layer {' +
'  marker-width: 1;' +
```

```
'   marker-fill: #b10026; ' +
'}';

var torqueLayer = new L.TorqueLayer({
    user: 'billkastanakis',
    table: "flights",
    cartocss: style,
    cumulative: true,
});
torqueLayer.addTo(map);
torqueLayer.play();
```

That's the *simplest* way to visualize torque data over time. We are going to explain how that code works, and we will enhance it after you've understood what's going on.

At this point, you can open `index.html` in a web browser to get a taste of what we have created so far:

We first create a CartoCSS string with the style that will be used in the map. Let's dissect that to understand what's going on in each part.

Torque uses a limited subset of CartoCSS, with some additional Torque-specific properties, which always begin with the keyword `-torque-`.

At `'-torque-time-attribute: "date";'` is where we specify the table field that contains the date data. As we mentioned in the previous section of the recipe, a string data type will not work, and it's often the reason for frustration. Make sure that you specify a valid table field name with a date data type.

At `'-torque-aggregation-function: "count(cartodb_id)";'` is where we define the function to aggregate data for each cell.

`'-torque-frame-count: 760;'` is the number of steps/frames. In this example, we use a single frame per row of data.

`'-torque-animation-duration: 5;'` means that the total duration is 5 seconds.

`'-torque-resolution: 2;'` is the spatial resolution in pixels. This value must be a power of 2. A value of 1 means no spatial aggregation at all. Imagine that property as *clustering*. A value of 2 means that the data will be clustered by two, while larger values will cluster more data.

Next we have code that styles the markers:

```
'#layer {' +
'   marker-width: 1;' +
'   marker-fill: #b10026; ' +
'}';
```

We use a width of 1 and fill color. That completes the code needed to style the Torque data.

In the next part, we simply create a new `torqueLayer`, and pass the values for the CartoDB user, the table, and the style fields that we have just created:

```
var torqueLayer = new L.TorqueLayer({
    user: 'billkastanakis',
    table: "flights",
    cartocss: style,
    cumulative: true,
});
```

Here, `cumulative: true` means that Torque will not clear the map at each frame. Instead, it will overlay the new data over the old one. If we try to set that to `false`, we will notice that the dots appear and disappear rather quickly. It may be hard to see this, but you can observe it easily if you set the `marker-width` attribute to a higher value.

In the next two lines, we simply add the `torqueLayer` to our map, and lastly, we add `torqueLayer.play();` to start playing the animation:

```
torqueLayer.addTo(map);
torqueLayer.play();
```

The next steps are as follows:

1. Now that we have created the basic functionality, we are going to enhance the styling of the Torque data. Replace the `style` variable with the following code:

```
var style =
  'Map {' +
  '-torque-time-attribute: "date";' +
  '-torque-aggregation-function: "count(cartodb_id)";' +
  '-torque-frame-count: 760;' +
  '-torque-animation-duration: 5;' +
  '-torque-resolution: 2' +
  '}' +
'#layer {' +
'  marker-width: 1;' +
'  marker-fill-opacity: 1;' +
'  marker-fill: #b10026; ' +
'  [value > 2] { marker-fill: #b10026; }' +
'  [value > 3] { marker-fill: #e31a1c; }' +
'  [value > 4] { marker-fill: #fc4e2a; }' +
'  [value > 5] { marker-fill: #fd8d3c; }' +
'  [value > 6] { marker-fill: #feb24c; }' +
'  [value > 7] { marker-fill: #fed976; }' +
'  [value > 8] { marker-fill: #ffffb2; }' +
'  [frame-offset = 1] { marker-width: 10; marker-fill-opacity:
0.05;}' +
'  [frame-offset = 2] { marker-width: 20; marker-fill-opacity:
0.02;}' +
'}';
```

In the preceding code, we use the following lines:

```
'  [value > 2] { marker-fill: #b10026; }' +
'  [value > 3] { marker-fill: #e31a1c; }' +
```

We are setting the marker color to change from red to a lighter yellow over time.

 We can also use the `zoom` variable to change the marker styling at different zoom levels.

Then, as shown in the following code, we set the two previous frames to a marker of width `10` with reduced opacity. This will create a glow effect:

```
'   [frame-offset = 1] { marker-width: 10; marker-fill-opacity:
0.05;}' +
'   [frame-offset = 2] { marker-width: 20; marker-fill-opacity:
0.02;}'
```

2. In the `torqueLayer` object, add a new property:

   ```
   blendmode: 'lighter',
   ```

   This property will give an intense *additive* compositing effect when a marker is above another marker.

    A great explanation of compositing operators can be found at `http://dev.w3.org/fxtf/compositing-1/#porterdu ffcompositingoperators`.

The following screenshot depicts the final result:

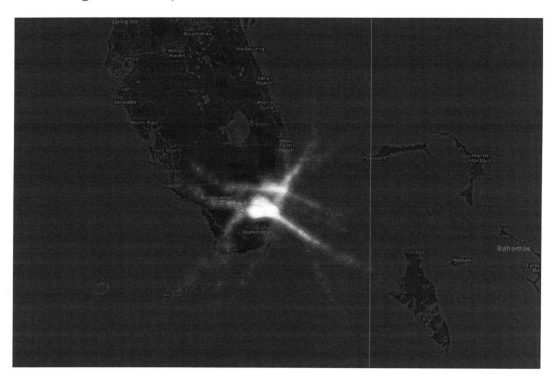

Comparing two maps at the same time

In this recipe, we are going to learn how to *compare* two maps at the same time. We can have two maps that are styled differently and which display different features. For example, one may use street data, while the other may use terrain or satellite imagery. The user will be able to swipe between the two maps.

How to do it...

The following steps need to be performed:

1. Add an HTML5 slider input control to the DOM.
2. Add an overlay map layer at the top of the base layer.
3. Calculate the clipping point based on the slider input value.
4. Create a `rect`, and apply that to the `clip` CSS property of the `map` container.

We first create an overlay map, and add it at the top of the base map. Next, we use a simple HTML5 input control, a *range* slider. As the user drags the slider, the overlay map gets clipped. All the magic happens in CSS. We have an overlay layer already in place, and we *clip* it based on the input value of the range slider. The CSS property that we are tweaking on slider change is called `clip`. The `clip` property accepts a rectangle, and we calculate that rectangle based on the map size on the screen and the input of the range slider.

Comparing two maps

Perform the following steps:

1. Start by opening the `chapter 5 - compare` folder in your favorite editor. In the `index.html` file, we will create an `<input>` field that will hold an HTML5 range slider control:

   ```
   <input id='range' class='range' type='range' min='0'
       max='1.0' step='any' />
   ```

2. Now head over to `main.js`. We already have a base map, but we also need an overlay layer to be at the top of the base map. This layer will hold the satellite map:

   ```
   var overlayLayer = L.mapbox.tileLayer
       ('mapboxrecipes.mjkd3a91').addTo(map);
   ```

3. Get the range input control from the DOM:

   ```
   var range = document.getElementById('range');
   ```

4. Now let's create the function that will clip the map:

   ```
   function clip(map, layer) {

       var nw = map.containerPointToLayerPoint([0, 0]);
       var se = map.containerPointToLayerPoint(map.getSize());
       var clipX = nw.x + (se.x - nw.x) * range.value;

       layer.getContainer().style.clip = 'rect(' + [nw.y, clipX,
           se.y, nw.x].join('px,') + 'px)';

   }
   ```

The first variable, nw, holds the northwest corner. It always points at 0,0. The next is the se variable where we use getSize(), which gets the size of the map container. With the third variable, called clipX, we do some math to find the position to clip the map at.

Finally, we apply style.clip to the container, which is just a CSS property. The clip CSS property accepts a rectangle, rect, and the values defined in the following order: top, right, bottom, and left. We pass the clipX value that we created earlier to the right value of the rectangle. px is attached as a suffix in each of the rect values. The final rect that is passed to the clip looks like this:

```
rect(0px,973.5px,767px,0px)
```

5. Now that the clip function is ready, we create two event handlers. The first one is range.onInput, which triggers whenever we change the value of the range input control:

```
range.oninput = function(e) {
  clip(map, overlayLayer)
}
```

6. The second one is on map move. Whenever we move the map, we need to update the clip CSS values:

```
map.on('move', function(e) {
  clip(map, overlayLayer)
});
```

7. Finally, we need to style the HTML slider input control, and position it at the top of the map. Open css/style.css, and add the following:

```
.range {
  position:absolute;
  width:100%;
}

input[type='range'] {
  -webkit-appearance: none !important;
  background: black;
  opacity: 0.75;
  height: 30px;
}

input[type='range']::-webkit-slider-thumb {
  -webkit-appearance: none !important;
  background:white;
  height: 50px;
  width: 15px;
}
```

That's all! Open `index.html` in your browser, and try to drag the map or the slider:

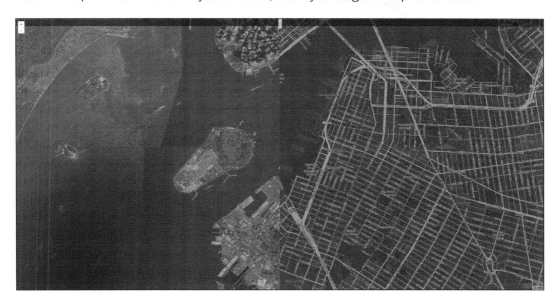

Adding a WMS layer from GeoServer to your map

In the previous recipe, we learned how to use CartoDB georeferenced data and draw it over time. In this recipe, we will learn how we can serve WMS layers using **GeoServer**.

While GeoServer is one of the most popular options, there are other great alternatives for publishing spatial data and interactive mapping applications, such as MapServer. You can find more information about MapServer at the official website at `http://mapserver.org`.

GeoServer is an open source server for serving geospatial data. WMS is georeferenced images used to display data that can't be easily represented using markers. An example is meteorological data such as clouds, winds, or surface heat maps.

How to do it...

The steps to be performed can be categorized in the following sections.

Adding WMS images from GeoServer to your map

First we will install GeoServer.

Installing GeoServer

We will first download and install GeoServer. It's freely available for Windows, Linux, and OS X. Both stable and nightly builds are available. I recommend that you download the stable build for this recipe:

1. Head over to `http://www.geoserver.org/release/stable` and download the installer for the operating system you're using.

2. Install the downloaded file. Instructions may differ between platforms, but usually, it is extremely easy to install it. You only need to run the downloaded installer. The installer will ask for the GeoServer port (I used `9876` in my setup) as well as the administrator password.

3. In case you've set up the installer to not start GeoServer automatically, you may need to start it manually. Again, the way to start it differs in various operating systems, but is pretty simple. On Windows, for example, there is a shortcut called **Start GeoServer**; if you installed it as a service, you may need to open **Services**, and start the GeoServer service.

> If you have trouble installing or starting GeoServer, the article at `http://docs.geoserver.org/stable/en/user/installation/index.html` contains instructions for all the available platforms.

4. Once installed and started, open a web browser, and head over to `http://localhost:9876/geoserver/web/`. Note that I am using `9876` as the port in my installation, but GeoServer defaults to the `8080` port. It's a good idea to change the port number during the installation process since `8080` is used by many different server applications.

5. Once you have access to the GeoServer web page, log in using the administrator credentials:

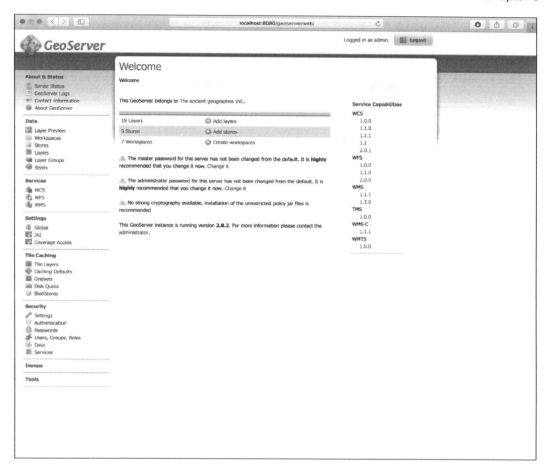

Creating a layer

Now that GeoServer is installed and running, we need to set it up to serve our data:

1. The first thing needed is to create a **workspace**. A workspace is used to group several layers or layer groups together. In the left sidebar, under **Data**, click on **Workspaces**. You will see that there is a list of workspaces set up already. Those are the default workspaces installed with GeoServer, but we are going to create our own.

2. Click on **Add New Workspace**, and give your workspace a name and a URI. I have named mine mapboxrecipes, and I have set the URI as http://www.mapboxrecipes.com/mapboxrecipes. As an optional step, you can go ahead and check the **Default Workspace** checkbox. When checked, any new stores or layers will automatically be created under the default workspace. Click on **Submit** once done:

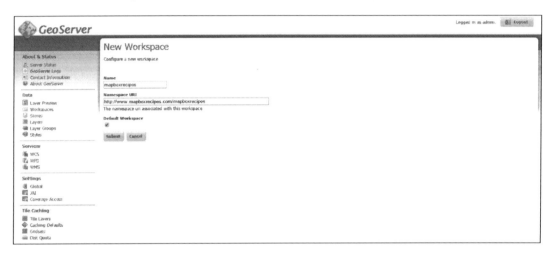

3. Now we need to add our data. In GeoServer, data is added as data sources under stores. A store can handle various types of vector and raster formats. We can load shapefiles (.shp), PostGIS databases, GeoTIFF, and several other formats.

   In this recipe, we are going to load cloud data to display over our Mapbox map. The data is in a GeoTIFF file.

   Click on **Stores** in the left sidebar, and then on **Add New Store**. From the list of supported data sources, choose **GeoTIFF**.

4. The workspace should already be set to **mapboxrecipes** since we have it as default. Give a name to your data source, and set a description if you wish. Make sure that the **Enabled** tab is checked. Once you have filled the required fields, click on **Browse** next to the **Connection Parameters** URL, and choose the GeoTIFF from your hard drive. Once done, click on **Save**.

When we save our newly-created store, we have the option to publish it. This creates a layer that is using that data source automatically.

5. If you didn't publish the store in the previous step, click on **Layers** in the left sidebar, and choose **Add New Resource**. From the **Add layer from** combo box, select **mapboxrecipes:clouds**. Click on **Publish**.

 GeoServer references our stores using `workspacename:storename`.

6. We have just created a new layer that is using the store we created earlier. To make sure that everything is correct, click on **Layer Preview** in the sidebar on the left, then find the layer we just created.

There are multiple ways to preview the layer. GeoServer gives us the option to render it to a file format such as JPG, GeoTIFF, PDF, KML, and many others, but in this case, we will preview it live by clicking on **OpenLayers** under **Common Formats**:

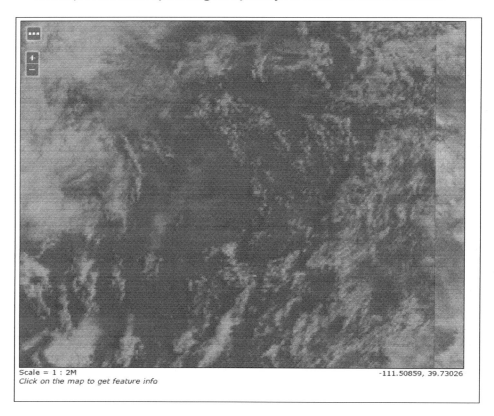

That's it. We have used GeoServer to create a new store that uses our data, and then a new layer.

Displaying WMS layers using Mapbox.js

The following steps need to be performed:

1. Go to the home page of the GeoServer interface at `http://localhost:9876/geoserver/web/` and copy the **1.3.0** link under **WMS**. That's the URL GeoServer uses to serve WMS.

2. Open the `chapter 5 - geoserver` folder in your favorite text editor, and head directly to `main.js`. As usual, the project is already set up to use a Mapbox base layer. After the `map` variable, type the following code:

```
var cloudLayer = L.tileLayer.wms('http://localhost:9876/
  geoserver/ows?service=wms&version=1.3.0&
  request=GetCapabilities', {
    layers: 'cloudscoverage',
    format: 'image/png',
    transparent: true
}).addTo(map);
```

We create `tileLayer.wms`, passing the URL we copied earlier from GeoServer.

At `layers:`, we pass the layer that uses our cloud coverage data. At `format:`, we request PNG files. And we set `transparent` to `true` in order for GeoServer to send us transparent PNGs.

3. Open `index.html` in your favorite browser to preview the map:

4. Great! The **WMS** layer is overlaid on top of the base map, but we are not able to see through the cloud layer.

5. Ideally, in case the tiles were transparent PNGs, there would be no issue at all since we are using `transparent: true`, but in this case, we have to do something more to complete the recipe.

    In the previous recipe, we used a slider input HTML5 element to drive the clipping of the map. We are going to do something similar here.

We will add a slider to drive the opacity of the WMS layer. Then we will be able to control the mix with the base map. This is not the ideal solution, but since the server is not returning transparent imagery, it's a perfectly valid way to visualize the cloud layer over the base map.

6. Open `index.html` and add a slider range input control:

    ```html
    <input id='range' class='range' type='range' min='0'
      max='1.0' step='any' />
    ```

7. Now open `main.js` and add the following code:

    ```javascript
    var range = document.getElementById('range');

    range.oninput = function(e) {
      cloudLayer.setOpacity(range.value);
    }
    ```

    It's similar to the previous recipe, with the only difference being that we now set the opacity of `cloudLayer` with `cloudLayer.setOpacity(range.value)`.

8. The last step is to position and style the HTML5 slider. Open `css/style.css` and add the following code:

    ```css
    .range {
      position:absolute;
      width:15%;
    }

    input[type='range'] {
      -webkit-appearance: none !important;
      background: black;
      opacity: 0.75;
      height: 10px;
      top: 20px;
      right: 20px;
    }

    input[type='range']::-webkit-slider-thumb {
      -webkit-appearance: none !important;
      background: white;
      height: 40px;
      width: 15px;
    }
    ```

That's all! Open `index.html` in your browser. Now you can use the slider to mix `cloudLayer` with the base map.

Adding ArcGIS layers from a server or from online

ArcGIS is a platform for making, using, and sharing maps from any device, anywhere, and at any time. This is how it's described on the ArcGIS website, and that's what it is, in a sentence.

Unlike QGIS, which we used in the previous chapters, ArcGIS is commercial software, and is a very deep and complex platform used by the GIS professionals.

 There is a 60-day free trial if you are interested in exploring ArcGIS; it is available at `http://www.esri.com/software/ arcgis/arcgis-for-desktop/free-trial`.

The platform is composed of several different applications, including ArcGIS Desktop in three different variations. It includes several applications, such as ArcMap, ArchToolbox, and others; it also includes ArcReader to view and query maps and ArcGIS Server to create and manage GIS web services, applications, and data.

Due to the complexity of the applications and server products, we are not going to dive deep into them since it would require a couple of books to cover them. If you're interested in learning more about ArcGIS, the following books by Packt Publishing will help you:

- *Administering ArcGIS for Server, Hussein Nasser* (`https://www.packtpub.com/networking-and-servers/administering-arcgis-server`)

- *ArcGIS for Desktop Cookbook, Daniela Christiana Docan* (`https://www.packtpub.com/application-development/arcgis-desktop-cookbook`)

- *Learning ArcGIS Geodatabases, Hussein Nasser* (`https://www.packtpub.com/application-development/learning-arcgis-geodatabases`)

Instead, we are going to create a recipe to learn how to access the data and layers created by ArcGIS, and combine them with Mapbox maps using Mapbox.js and a Leaflet plugin. ArcGIS has its own JavaScript API; the plugin we are going to use is not going to replace it, but will help us combine ArcGIS technology with the Mapbox data we are using.

 If you want to explore the ArcGIS API, the documentation can be found at `https://developers.arcgis.com/javascript/`.

How to do it...

The following steps need to be performed:

1. Publish your own service using ArcGIS or use an online service. Acquire the URL from the service.
2. Link the **Esri Leaflet** plugin to your project.
3. Open the URL and explore the layers and properties provided by the service.
4. Use `esri.TileLayer` and pass the URL. Add the layer to the map.
5. Generate an on-click event listener.
6. Create an `L.esri.Tasks.IdentifyFeatures` request to acquire the features at the clicked latitude and longitude.
7. Parse the returned `featureCollection`, generate an HTML, and create a popup to display the data.

In ArcGIS, you can create your maps using the ArcGIS Desktop ArcMap software. The process is similar to the maps we created in the previous chapters using QGIS. They are composited by layers and various types of datasets.

After the map is created, a service can be created using the ArcGIS Server software. The map can be published using the service and shared with the world.

To get that data from the service, we have to use a Leaflet plugin called Esri Leaflet. It will help us connect to the services and acquire the data we want easily. Esri Leaflet is an excellent plugin and it can do a lot more. In the recipe, we will use a limited set of the functionality provided by it, but with the knowledge acquired in this chapter, it will be easy enough to get the most out of it without any trouble.

Adding ArcGIS layers from the server or from online

Perform these steps:

1. We are going to use the services available in the ArcGIS Services directory. Head over to it and click on the **Demographics** folder, then on **Demographics/USA_2000-2010_Population_Change (MapServer)**.

   A screen with the details will appear. It includes information about the layers used in the server as well as details about the tiles and the supported operations:

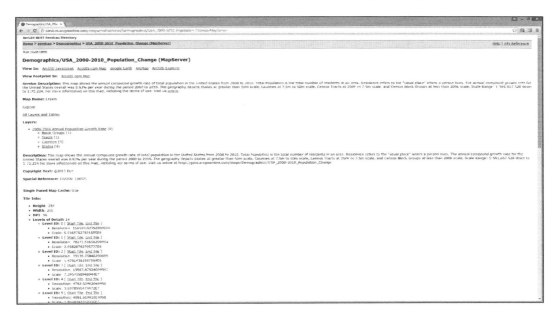

There are multiple ways to preview the data. At the top of the page, there are several **View In** options. Clicking on **ArcGIS.com Map** will open the map in your browser directly:

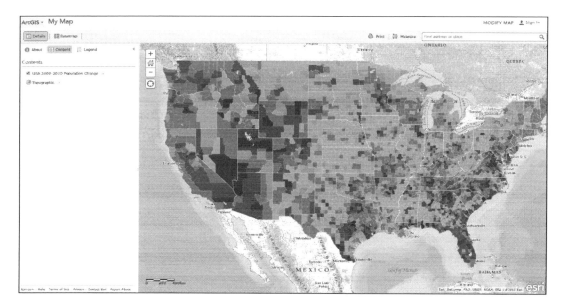

If you have ArcMap installed on your machine, you can click on **ArcMap** in the **View In** options. It will download a `.lyr` (layer) file, which you can double-click on to open it in ArcMap.

 Don't confuse a shape file (`.shp`) with an ArcGIS layer file. The latter doesn't actually hold any data, but just a reference path to the source dataset.

Inside ArcMap, you can get information about the layers that the service contains, and explore its features and properties:

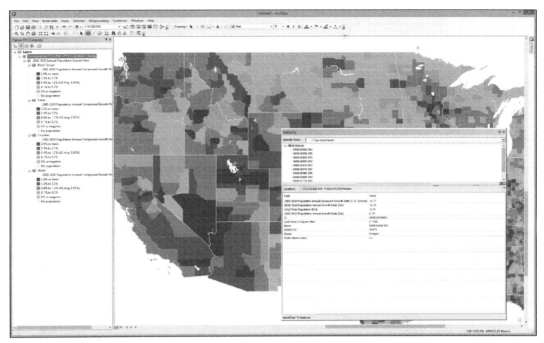

In this instance, the service contains four layers: the **Block Groups** at index 1, the **Tracts** at index 2, **Counties** at index 3, and **States** at index 4.

If you click on the **States** or **Counties** layers on the ArcGIS Services directory page or in ArcMap, you will see that they contain fields such as the name of the state, land area in square miles, as well as the growth by year ranges.

We are going to display this data in a popup later.

2. Now that we have an understanding of the data that is supplied by the service, it's time to dive into our project. Open the folder `chapter 5 - esri` in your favorite HTML editor. The project contains a basic setup like the previous recipes. In this recipe, we are going to use Esri Leaflet. It will help us with loading Esri base maps and feature services as well as tile, dynamic maps, and image services.

3. Open `index.html` and add the following line to link to the Esri Leaflet plugin:

    ```
    <script src="//cdn.jsdelivr.net/leaflet.esri/
        latest/esri-leaflet.js"></script>
    ```

4. Let's jump into the `js/main.js` file. We will first create a `url` variable. The address will be the same as the services address that we used earlier:

```
var url = demographicsURL = "http://
    services.arcgisonline.com/arcgis/rest/services/
    Demographics/USA_2000-2010_Population_Change/MapServer";
```

5. Next we will add an Esri tile layer to the map. As a parameter, we just supply the preceding `url`:

```
var layer = L.esri.tiledMapLayer(demographicsURL,
    {}).addTo(map);
```

6. Create an on-click event handler. We want to identify the features each time the user clicks on the map:

```
map.on('click', function(e) {

});
```

7. Within the on-click context, add the following code:

```
L.esri.Tasks.identifyFeatures({
    url: url
})
.on(map)
.at(e.latlng)
.layers('States')
.run(function(error, featureCollection, response){
    // Add code to parse the featureCollection and
        response
}

});
```

Here, we call the `identifyFeatures` method from the Esri Leaflet plugin. We pass `map` and `latlng` from the on-click handler. In the `layers` parameter, we pass one of the layers provided by the service. We saw that they were four layers, of which one was the `States` layer.

The last part is `run`, which executes the `identifyFeatures` request.

8. Within the `run` function context, after the `// add code to parse...` comment, add the following code to generate a popup where the user clicks:

```
if (response.results.length > 0) {

    var properties = featureCollection.features[0].
        properties;
    var html =   '<h1>' + properties['Name'] + '</h1>' +
```

```
                          '<small>Square miles: ' +
properties['Land Area in Square Miles'] + '</small>' +
                          '<p><strong>Population: </strong>' +
properties['2010 Total Population (U.S. Census)'] + '</p>' +
                          '<p><strong>2000-2010 growth: </
strong>' + properties['2000-2010 Population Annual Compound Growth
Rate (U.S. Census)'] + '</p>' +
                          '<p><strong>2010-2012 growth: </
strong>' + properties['2010-2012 Population: Annual Growth Rate
(Esri)'] + '</p>' +
                          '<p><strong>2012-2017 growth: </
strong>' + properties['2012-2017 Population: Annual Growth Rate
(Esri)'] + '</p>';

        var popup = L.popup()
        .setLatLng(e.latlng)
        .setContent(html)
        .openOn(map);

    }
```

What we are doing here is parsing: getting the data we want from `featureCollection`, generating an HTML variable, and passing that to the popup, like in the previous recipes. And you may ask, how do we know which fields are returned in `featureCollection`?

You can go to `console.log` and find out, or simply open the service URL in your browser and the fields are provided at the bottom of the page under the **States** layer.

The following is what you will see:

Fields:

OBJECTID (type: esriFieldTypeOID , alias: OBJECTID)

Shape (type: esriFieldTypeGeometry , alias: Shape)

ID (type: esriFieldTypeString , alias: ID , length: 2)

NAME (type: esriFieldTypeString , alias: Name , length: 20)

ST_ABBREV (type: esriFieldTypeString , alias: State Abbreviation , length: 2)

LANDAREA (type: esriFieldTypeDouble , alias: Land Area in Square Miles)

TOTPOP_CY (type: esriFieldTypeInteger , alias: 2012 Total Population (Esri))

TOTPOP10 (type: esriFieldTypeInteger , alias: 2010 Total Population (U.S. Census))

POPGRW0010 (type: esriFieldTypeDouble , alias: 2000-2010 Population Annual Compound Growth Rate (U.S. Census))

POPGRW10CY (type: esriFieldTypeDouble , alias: 2010-2012 Population: Annual Growth Rate (Esri))

POPGRWCYFY (type: esriFieldTypeDouble , alias: 2012-2017 Population: Annual Growth Rate (Esri))

That's it. We have managed to overlay ArcGIS layers over our own Mapbox base layer, and get information from the tiles, with just a few lines of code.

Open `index.html` in your web browser to see the final result. Try clicking on a state to open the demographics information popup:

Adding Fusion Tables to your map

Google Fusion Tables is a web service provided by Google for creating, visualizing, and sharing data tables. The data is stored in tables that the users can view, copy, combine, manipulate, and download.

In this recipe, we are going to combine two different Fusion Tables to get the data we want, then we will see how we can access the data and populate a Mapbox base map.

How to do it...

The following steps are required:

1. Generate a new Fusion Table, or use public data.

2. Get a Fusion Table API key for Google Developer Console.

3. Generate a SQL query to get the data you want from the Fusion Tables.

4. Use the Fusion Tables JavaScript API to send the request.

5. Parse the response, and populate the map.

Google calls Fusion Tables an *experimental* application, although that status has existed for several years now. The web application provides functionality for visualizing the data on a map or by using various types of chart such as bar charts, line plots, scatter plots, timelines, and so on. The data tables can be generated from Google Sheets, or imported from various file formats, such as `.csv`, `.tsv`, `.kml`, and others. While it's not a relational database, it is pretty similar since there is a functionality to combine various Fusion Tables into one. To access the data, we will need a Fusion Tables API key from Google Developer Console. Then we can use the Fusion Tables API to query the tables using the Fusion Tables JavaScript API and get the data we want. Once we have the data, we will use Mapbox.js to populate a base map.

Acquiring a Fusion Tables API key

We will need an API key to be able to use the JavaScript API:

1. Head over to `https://console.developers.google.com/project` and create a project, or use an existing one.

2. Once in the project, click on **API Manager** in the left sidebar.

3. You will find **Fusion Tables API** at the bottom under the **Other popular APIs** section. Click on it.

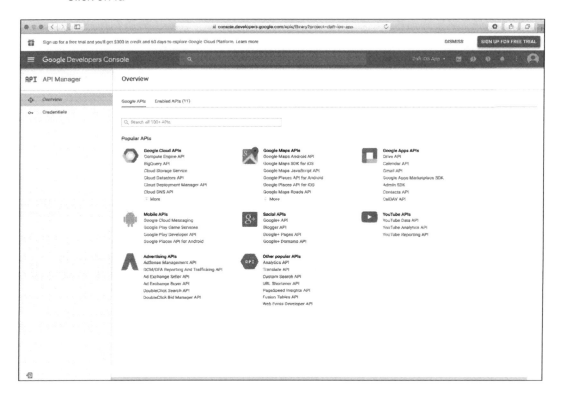

4. Click on **Enable**.

5. Go to the **Credentials** section in the sidebar.

6. Click on **Create credentials** and then on **API key**.

7. Select **Browser key**, and click on **Create**.

8. Keep a note of the API key since we are going to use it later in the recipe.

Creating a Fusion Table

Fusion Tables can be created from scratch using spreadsheets, but there is data available publicly too. In this recipe, we are going to use two different public data Fusion Tables. We will merge their content to create a third one that has the *combined* data:

1. Head over to `https://research.google.com/tables`. From here you can make a query, and search for the data you want. There are two options in the sidebar, **Web Tables** and **Fusion Tables**. Web tables are, as you've probably already guessed, tabular data inside `<table></table>` tags. When you are searching, make sure that **Fusion Tables** is selected here.

   The first table we are going to use is *crime statistics by postcode* in England and Wales. The table can be found at the following link: `https://www.google.com/fusiontables/DataSource?docid=1Nu5cyP1ulEWNilmZCgF4axei56fT8c IV7-wutK8#rows:id=1`.

   Note that this is a public table, and it may not be available at the time you're reading this recipe. You can search for a table that contains crime statistics, and also includes a postcode, or a city name, or even latitude and longitude. Any table like that will work just fine to get you through the recipe.

   Note that the table has a postcode, but no actual latitude and longitude columns. This is where the second table comes in. It will help us map the postcode to the location coordinates.

   If you want to import your own data, or create a new Fusion Table from scratch, the process is extremely easy.

   Just head to the **File** menu, and choose **New table...**. Here you will have the option to load `.csv`, `.tsv`, `.txt`, or `.kml` files from your computer, import from Google Sheets, or create an empty table.

2. Before taking a look at the other table, let's copy the Fusion Table into our account first. Go to **File**, and choose **Make a copy**. After a few seconds, the table will be copied into our account.

12. Since we are here, let's get the ID for the table. We are going to use the ID to link to this table when using the Fusion Tables API.

There are two ways to get the ID. The first one is just by inspecting the URL, which is `https://www.google.com/fusiontables/data?docid=1pt-ezE2tlDLKP6M bcQFP5GjLqa6tugMUqSHakSTo#rows:id=1`.

The data after `docid=` until the `hash` character is the ID of the table. In this case, it is `1pt-ezE2tlDLKP6MbcQFP5GjLqa6tugMUqSHakSTo`.

The other way is to click on **File**, then choose **About this table**. The ID of the table is at the bottom end of this About box.

That's it. We have now generated a new public Fusion Table from public data. Next, you are going to learn how to present that data in our maps using Mapbox.js.

Adding Fusion Tables data to your map

Perform the following steps:

1. Open the `chapter 5 - fusionTables` folder in your favorite text editor.

2. The first function that we are going to create is the request to the Fusion Tables API:

```
function requestData() {

  var fusionTablesAPIKey = "AIzaSyBidVY6GUVnQE2cmpq_
phTZJ37ModYJKPE";
  var fusionTableID = '1BQkBcXZ4F_hDVs6uQUzKCfJ-CXN_eJnfFSuiCZFv';

  var query = encodeURIComponent("SELECT 'Postcode District',
AVERAGE('Estimated Population'), latitude, longitude, SUM('Violent
Crime Total'), SUM('Shoplifting Total'), SUM('Drugs Total'),
SUM('Public Disorder and Weapons Total'), SUM('Criminal Damage
and Arson Total') FROM " + fusionTableID + " GROUP BY 'Postcode
District', latitude, longitude");
  var url = 'https://www.googleapis.com/fusiontables/
v2/query?sql=' + query + '&key=' + fusionTablesAPIKey +
'&typed=false&callback=jsonp';
  var encodedURL = encodeURIComponent(url);

  $.ajax({
    url: url,
    dataType: 'jsonp',
    jsonpCallback: 'jsonp',
    success: parseFusionTableResponse,
    error: errorResponse
  });

}
```

The first part in this function is the `query` variable. We construct an SQL query to fetch the data that we want.

You have probably noticed that we are also using aggregate functions to count and average several rows:

```
var query = encodeURIComponent("SELECT 'Postcode District',
AVERAGE('Estimated Population'), latitude, longitude, SUM('Violent
Crime Total'), SUM('Shoplifting Total'), SUM('Drugs Total'),
SUM('Public Disorder and Weapons Total'), SUM('Criminal Damage
and Arson Total') FROM " + fusionTableID + " GROUP BY 'Postcode
District', latitude, longitude");
```

What we are basically doing in the preceding query is grouping the results to have the summaries that we need.

The Fusion Tables API supports the `SELECT`, `INSERT`, `UPDATE`, and `DELETE` SQL clauses. We use `SELECT` here, and it supports the `WHERE`, `GROUP BY`, `ORDER BY`, `OFFSET`, and `LIMIT` clauses. The aggregate functions supported are `COUNT`, `SUM`, `AVERAGE`, `MAXIMUM`, and `MINIMUM`.

> You can find more information for the `SELECT` clause in the Fusion Tables API documentation at `https://developers.google.com/fusiontables/docs/v2/sql-reference#Select`.

Note `FROM " + fusionTableID`. The table name is the Fusion Table ID we got earlier.

Make a note here about what is supported when generating your SQL query so that you don't get any unexpected results or errors from the Fusion Tables API.

The SQL statement has to go through `encodeURIComponent()` to encode special characters.

After the SQL statement is constructed, we generate the URL to query the API:

```
var url = 'https://www.googleapis.com/fusiontables/v2/
   query?sql=' + query + '&key=' + fusionTablesAPIKey +
   '&typed=false&callback=jsonp';
var encodedURL = encodeURIComponent(url);
```

Our Google `fusionTablesAPIKey` that we got from Google Developers Console is passed here.

Once `url` is ready, we use jQuery AJAX to call the API:

```
$.ajax({
      url: url,
      dataType: 'jsonp',
      jsonpCallback: 'jsonp',
      success: parseFusionTableResponse,
      error: errorResponse
});
```

In case we get a response, the `success` callback will be called, and that's what we are going to do now.

3. We generate a function to parse the results from the Fusion Tables API. The function will enumerate through the results, and it will create markers for each row. The markers will be added to a new layer called `crimeLayer`:

```
function parseFusionTableResponse(data) {

    L.mapbox.accessToken = 'pk.eyJ1IjoibWFwYm94cmVja
        XBlcyIsImEiOiJjd3RhQmlzIn0.Wx0fWGCo3gs6fzta5QrLfw';
    var mapboxTiles = L.tileLayer('https://{s}.tiles.
        mapbox.com/v4/mapboxrecipes.mb2jjne3/{z}/{x}/{y}.png?
        access_token=' + L.mapbox.accessToken);

    var latlong = [51.5072, 0.1257];
    var map = L.map('map').addLayer(mapboxTiles).
        setView(latlong, 8);
    var crimeLayer = L.layerGroup().addTo(map);

    for (var i = 0; i < data.rows.length; i++) {

        var entry = data.rows[i];
        var html = generateHTMLForEntry(entry);

        if (entry[2] != "" || entry[3] != "") {

            var latlng = L.latLng(entry[2], entry[3]);

            var marker = L.marker(latlng, {
                icon: L.mapbox.marker.icon({
                    'marker-color': '#d40000',
                    'marker-symbol': 'danger',
                    'marker-size': 'large'
                })

            }).bindPopup(html).addTo(crimeLayer);
        }

    }

}
```

This function is pretty similar to the one in the previous recipe, so not much explanation is needed.

In the first few lines of the function, we create a base map and an extra layer called `crimeLayer`. Then we loop through the results, generating markers and adding them to `crimeLayer`.

4. The last piece of the puzzle is to generate the HTML content of the markers:

```
function generateHTMLForEntry(entry) {

    var html = '<p><strong>Postcode: </strong>' + entry[0] + '<p>' +
               '<p><strong>Population: </strong>' + entry[1] + '<p>'
+
               '<p><strong>Violent Crimes Total: </strong>' +
entry[4] + '<p>' +
               '<p><strong>Shoplifting Total: </strong>' + entry[5]
+ '<p>' +
               '<p><strong>Drugs Total: </strong>' + entry[6] +
'<p>' +
            '<p><strong>Public Disorder & Weapons Total: </strong>'
+ entry[7] + '<p>' +
               '<p><strong>Criminal Damages Total: </strong>' +
entry[8] + '<p>';

    return html;
}
```

5. Don't forget the `onLoad` function to call `requestData()`:

```
window.onload = function() {
    requestData();
}
```

6. That's it. Open `index.html` in your favorite text editor:

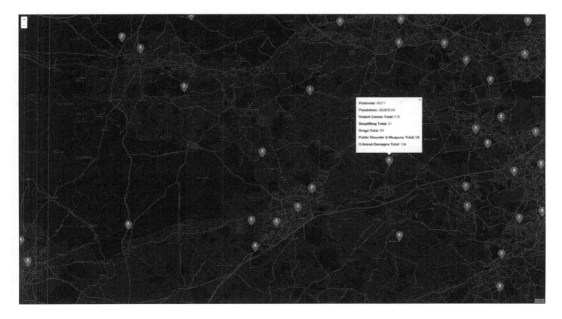

Adding Foursquare data to your map

In this recipe, we are going to learn how to use the Foursquare API, and populate a Mapbox base map with Foursquare data. We are going to populate the map with venues as we pan and zoom.

How to do it...

The following steps need to be performed:

1. Create a developer account at Foursquare.

2. Create a new app to get your client ID and client secret.

3. Construct a request to the Foursquare venues endpoint. Make sure that you are passing either the latitude and longitude using the `ll` parameter, or a city with the `near` parameter.

   The `query` parameter with a venue category, and the `v` parameter for the API versioning are also required.

4. Once the request is constructed, use jQuery's `getJSON` function to call the endpoint.

5. Enumerate through the returned results, and for each venue, create a new marker.

6. Add all the markers to a new layer, and add the layer to the map.

Foursquare has a public API that is free to use as long as you have a developer account. It's a RESTful API, and using the available endpoints, you can get information about venues, users, check-ins, events, and much more. Since it's a kind of a headache to perform CORS requests using JavaScript, we will recruit jQuery to help us with the API network requests. Once we get back a response, we will enumerate through the results, and for each one, we will create a marker on the map.

Getting Foursquare data to your map

Perform these steps:

1. First of all, we will need an account to use the Foursquare API. Head over to `https://developer.foursquare.com`, and log in with your credentials or sign up for a new account.

2. The next step is to create a new app to use for this recipe. Click on **My Apps** from the top menu, then on **Create a new app**. Give your app an app name; you will also need to fill in the **Web addresses** sections with the URLs of your app. We are not going to use them, and it isn't important to use real URLs for the purpose of this recipe.

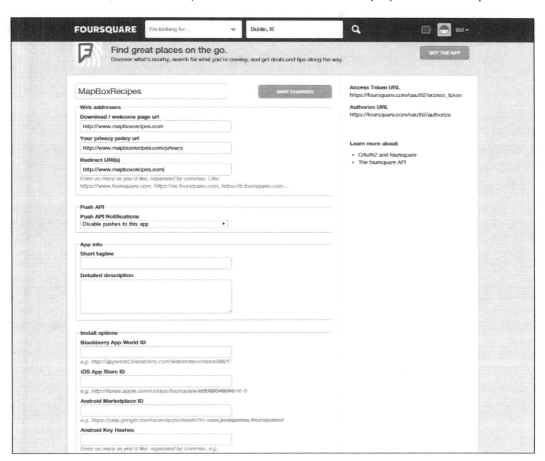

3. Once your app is created, Foursquare will display your app's client ID and client secret. We will need those to get access to the API.

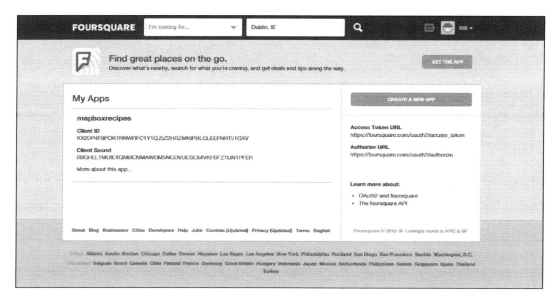

4. Fire up your favorite text editor and open the `chapter 5 - foursquare` folder. The project is already set up to use a Mapbox base map.

5. In this project, we are going to use the jQuery `getJSON` function to make it easier to talk to the Foursquare API. We will need to link to jQuery, so add the following line to your `index.html` file:

    ```
    <script src='https://code.jquery.com/jquery-1.11.0.
       min.js'></script>
    ```

6. Open `main.js`. To make the project easier to read, we are going to create several functions. The first is called `requestData(map, layer)`, and it will be used to generate the Foursquare API request:

    ```
    function requestData(map, layer) {

      var clientID = 'KX2DP4F0POK1RNWRFC1Y1QJ5Z2HRZMKIPBL
        CLEEFNRT51GXV';
      var clientSecret = '0BGHLLTMUIEXQMBCNMAWDM5NGDV
        UESEX4VKFBFZ1IJN1PFER';

      var url = 'https://api.foursquare.com/v2/venues/search' +
          '?client_id=' + clientID +
          '&client_secret=' + clientSecret +
          '&v=20150714' +
    ```

```
                '&limit=50' +
                '&radius=100000' +
                '&ll=' + map.getCenter().lat + ',' + map.getCenter().lng +
                '&query=restaurant';

            $.getJSON(url, function(results, status) {

                if (status !== 'success') return alert('Request
                Failed');
                    parseResults(layer, results);

            });

        }
```

We use the `venues/search` endpoint to search for venues. Let's dissect the preceding code.

In the first two lines, we create two variables to store the client ID and client secret:

```
                '?client_id=' + clientID +
                '&client_secret=' + clientSecret +
```

We pass a date to the parameter v. This is related to API versioning. It is a required parameter, and the numbers next to it are simply a date in the *YYYY/MM/DD* format. It means that Foursquare will use the latest API version available on that date, as shown here:

```
                '&v=20150614'   +
```

In the next two lines, we set the limit to return 50 venues, which is the maximum, and the radius of the search is to be 100.000 meters:

```
                '&limit=50' +
                '&radius=100000' +
```

The other required parameters for this endpoint are `ll` or `near`. One or the other is required, but you can't use both. The first one, `ll`, is used to pass the longitude and latitude to search, and `near` is used to search near a specific address or city. In this case, we use `ll`, and pass the center of the map as the longitude and latitude values:

```
                '&ll=' + map.getCenter().lat + ',' +
                    map.getCenter().lng +
```

Lastly, we pass the venues we are looking for, such as sushi, restaurant, or café, to the `query` parameter :

```
                '&query=restaurant';
```

Once the request URL has been constructed, we use jQuery's `getJSON` function to call the endpoint:

```
$.getJSON(url, function(results, status) {

    if (status !== 'success') return alert('Request
      Failed');
    parseResults(layer, results);

});
```

It will give us back `results`, which are venue objects, and a status. If we don't get a `'success'` status, we display an alert with the error.

If the request returns `results`, we will create a function to parse those results.

7. For the moment, let's create a quick function to help us generate the HTML that we will display in the popups:

```
function generateHTMLForVenue(venue) {

    var html = '<h2><a href="https://foursquare.com/v/' + venue.id +
'">' + venue.name + '</a></h2>' +
              '<h4>' + venue.categories[0].name + '</h4>' +
              '<p>' + venue.location.address + ', ' + venue.
location.city + '</p>' +
              '<p>CheckIns: <strong>' + venue.stats.checkinsCount +
'</strong></p>';

    return html;
}
```

This function is self-explanatory, and simply generates an HTML using data from the returned venue objects. It displays a venue name that links to the Foursquare page, then the category, the address, and the number of check-ins. We will use this function next.

8. Now we are going to create the `parseResults(layer, results)` function:

```
function parseResults(layer, results) {

    for (var i = 0; i < results.response.venues.length;
      i++) {

    var venue = results.response.venues[i];
```

```
    var html = generateHTMLForVenue(venue);

    var latlng = L.latLng(venue.location.lat, venue.
      location.lng);

    var marker = L.marker(latlng, {
      icon: L.mapbox.marker.icon({
        'marker-color': '#d40000',
        'marker-symbol': 'restaurant',
        'marker-size': 'large'
      })
    }).bindPopup(html).addTo(layer);
  }


}
```

Let's dissect the function. We enumerate through `results.response.venues`, and create three variables: one to hold the venue, one to generate the HTML for the popup using the helper function that we created earlier, and one that stores the latitude and longitude:

```
var venue = results.response.venues[i];
var html = generateHTMLForVenue(venue);
var latlng = L.latLng(venue.location.lat, venue.
      location.lng);
```

Next, for each venue, we create a marker, pass `latlng`, and customize the marker to be red, have the restaurant icon, and be large in size:

```
var marker = L.marker(latlng, {
  icon: L.mapbox.marker.icon({
    'marker-color': '#d40000',
    'marker-symbol': 'restaurant',
    'marker-size': 'large'
  })
}).bindPopup(html).addTo(layer);
```

We also bind a popup with the HTML that we generated earlier. Finally, we add each marker to the layer, which will hold all of our Foursquare markers.

9. We are almost done. We just need to create the layer that will hold the Foursquare markers, and call the `requestData` function. We will do that in `window.onload = function()`:

```
var foursquareLayer = L.layerGroup().addTo(map);
requestData(map, foursquareLayer);
```

10. Let's do something even cooler. Let's add an event to add more data when the user is zooming or panning the map. The Mapbox `moveend` event handler is perfect for that:

```
map.on('moveend', function(e) {
  requestData(map, foursquareLayer);
});
```

11. Foursquare requires attribution. Let's comply with that, and add an attribution to thank them for providing their data to us:

```
map.attributionControl.addAttribution('Data powered by
Foursquare');
```

12. Save the file, and open `index.html` in your favorite browser. Try to scroll or zoom around, and click on the markers to see the information about the venues:

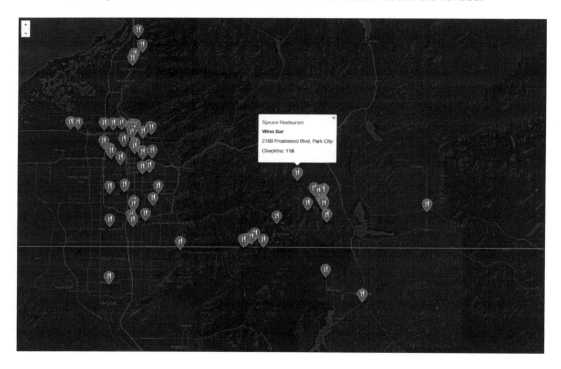

6
Mapbox GL

In this chapter, we will cover the following recipes:

- ▸ Integrating your project with Mapbox GL
- ▸ Creating a basic map using Mapbox GL
- ▸ Switching between locations programmatically
- ▸ Adding markers to the map
- ▸ Switching map styles
- ▸ Loading GeoJSON and drawing a polyline
- ▸ Drawing polygons on the map

Introduction

When I started writing this book, the best way to use Mapbox maps on the iOS platform was the **Mapbox iOS** SDK. While the SDK itself was pretty powerful, it was based on raster tiles and was significantly slower that modern vector map frameworks such as the Apple-owned MapKit. There were other disadvantages too; for example, it was messy to integrate into a project and generated tons of warnings.

 Don't confuse the Mapbox GL mobile framework with Mapbox GL JS, which is aimed at web developers. All the recipes in this chapter are for Mapbox GL iOS.

Luckily for us, Mapbox introduced a new mobile SDK that replaced the now deprecated Mapbox iOS SDK. It's called Mapbox GL, and it has significant strengths compared to its predecessor. Mapbox GL is written in C++, based on the OpenGL ES 2.0 technology, and is capable of displaying pixel-perfect vector maps without antialiasing or blurring issues. It's hardware accelerated and optimized for mobile hardware.

I considered introducing both frameworks in this chapter, but as the Mapbox iOS SDK is now deprecated, it would be a waste to start learning it now. Instead, I have chosen to dedicate this chapter to Mapbox GL, which will be the obvious choice for the future.

In the first recipe, we will create a basic app that displays a map on the screen. In the following recipes, we will explore how to zoom and pan the map programmatically, load predefined and custom styles, and draw markers and polygons.

Let's begin by integrating Mapbox GL into our project. This chapter is a significant step from the previous ones and uses a totally different language and tools. To be able to follow this chapter, knowledge of **Objective-C** or **Swift** as well as **Xcode** is required. Additionally, Mapbox GL uses raw C language features, such as structs, so knowledge of C will also help. You must be able to navigate by yourself in Xcode and understand how to get around.

In the first few recipes, I will try to be as detailed as possible so that users that don't have experience with iOS development have a chance to follow the recipes. However, if you have zero experience with iOS development and have trouble following the steps to complete the recipes, I strongly recommend that you read a beginner's guide that specializes in iOS development before attempting to follow the recipes.

Integrating your project with Mapbox GL

In this recipe, we will discover how you can integrate your projects with Mapbox GL.

How to do it...

The easiest way to link to external libraries or frameworks on the iOS platform is via **CocoaPods**. It's the most popular package manager and is built with Ruby, which is preinstalled in OS X. Also, installing it is extremely easy, as shown:

1. Open a terminal.
2. Paste the following command:

   ```
   sudo gem install cocoapods
   ```

3. After a few moments, CocoaPods will be installed. To make sure that everything is working, you can check the version via the following command:

   ```
   pod -version
   ```

   We will get back something similar to this:

   ```
   0.37.2
   ```

You can learn more about CocoaPods at `https://cocoapods.org`.

Creating the Xcode project file and linking it to Mapbox GL

Perform the following steps:

1. Open Xcode, and from the templates, select **Single View Application**.

 If you don't have Xcode installed, you can download it for free from the Mac App Store at `https://itunes.apple.com/us/app/xcode/id497799835?ls=1&mt=12`.

Before moving on, let's have a quick look at the Xcode user interface. If you are already familiar with Xcode, feel free to proceed to Step 3.

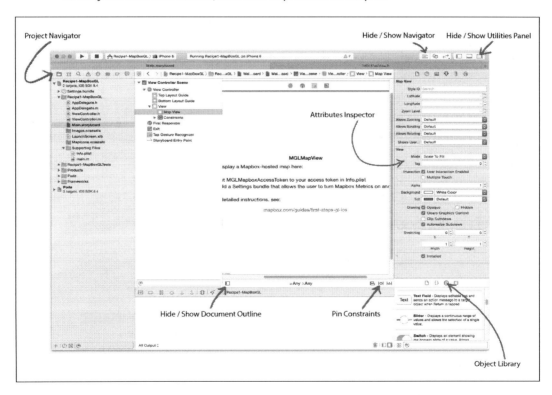

Project Navigator displays your projects and the files contained in each of your projects. You will see your source code classes there, as well as storyboards and other resources such as image files. You will even find external files that we want our project to have access to, such as GeoJSON. The **storyboard** is a file that contains the user interface elements and their layout for an app. It can contain multiple controllers, and how these controllers are connected to each other defines the flow of the app. The **Utilities Panel** displays information depending on which file we selected in **Project Navigator**. If a source file is selected in **File Inspector**, **Quick Help** is displayed. If a storyboard is selected, then **Attributes Inspector**, **Identity Inspector**, and others are displayed. The **Pin** button is used when you have a user interface element selected to add **AutoLayout** constraints. They define how the layout appears on screens of different sizes, such as on an iPhone or an iPad. **Documents Outline** is visible only when you have a storyboard selected. It shows the elements contained in the storyboard in a hierarchical manner.

Let's continue with the recipe.

2. Give your project a name and make sure that **Objective-C** is selected as the language. We will use Objective-C throughout the book instead of Swift due to the fact that Swift is still evolving too quickly and will probably break the recipes.

3. Select a folder for your project and take note of the folder location. We will need to navigate to this folder using the terminal in the next steps.

4. Click on **Create** to create your project.

5. Now that the project is created, you can close Xcode.

We will use CocoaPods to link Mapbox GL to our project, and after this, we need to open the workspace created by CocoaPods instead of the project file that is open now.

 If you feel confused with the project and workspace terminologies in Xcode, an easy way to explain it is that a workspace contains multiple projects. In this case, our workspace will contain our project and the Mapbox GL project.

6. Next, we need to open the terminal and use cd to go to our newly created project. In my case, I typed the following command:

```
cd projects/mapboxrecipes/Recipe1-MapBoxGL
```

7. We will create a Podfile for CocoaPods. The Podfile contains information about which libraries or frameworks are linked in our project. The Podfile must be in the root folder of our project. As we are already in this location, let's create the file as follows:

```
nano Podfile
```

8. The Nano text editor will open with an empty text file. Type the following text:

```
platform :ios, "7.0"
pod 'MapboxGL'
use_frameworks!
```

The first line, `platform :ios, "7.0"`, means that the minimum iOS version supported in our project is 7.0. Next, we will link to Mapbox GL using `pod 'MapboxGL'`. Finally, the `use_frameworks!` flag tells CocoaPods to integrate your project using frameworks instead of static libraries.

9. To save the Podfile in the Nano editor, hit *Ctrl + O* and then *Enter*.

10. Exit Nano by pressing *Ctrl + X*.

11. The Podfile is created, and now we need to tell CocoaPods to download the dependencies specified in the Podfile and link them to our project. Execute the following command:

```
pod install
```

The terminal will display a handful of information messages as the dependencies are being installed. If all the messages are green, then we are good to go. The messages should end with an important piece of information such as the following:

[!] Please close any current Xcode sessions and use `Recipe1-MapBoxGL.xcworkspace` for this project from now on.

As we explained earlier, opening the `.project` file in Xcode will not work because we are now linked with external projects. We will have to open the `.xcworkspace` file instead.

12. Open the `.xcworkspace` file. It can be found in your project's root folder in Xcode.

13. Go to the `ViewController.m` file. We need to import Mapbox GL. Add the following line after `#import "ViewController.h"`:

```
@import MapboxGL;
```

14. Build the project by hitting *Cmd + B*. If you get a successful message, then our project is linked correctly.

Creating a basic map using Mapbox GL

In this recipe, you will learn how to create basic maps with the help of Mapbox GL.

How to do it...

Now that we have integrated Mapbox GL into our project, it's time to learn the basics of the framework. In this recipe, we will create a basic app that shows a Mapbox GL map on screen. Here are the steps:

1. We will continue from the last step of the previous recipe after we have successfully linked and built our new project.

   Open the `Main.storyboard` file. Storyboards allow us to visually create user interfaces. The current storyboard already contains `ViewController`. We will add a new `MGLMapView`.

2. Make sure that the Utilities sidebar is visible. If not, click on the Hide or Show Utilities button in the upper-right corner of Xcode. In the lower half of the Utilities sidebar, make sure that Objects are selected.

   A list of the available UI elements will be visible. Find `UIView` and drag it into `UIViewController` in the storyboard. As you drag `UIView`, you will notice that guides appear to help you align the element. Make sure that `UIView` is centered and fills the whole screen before releasing the mouse button:

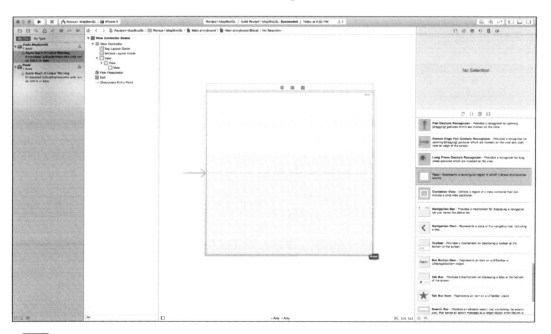

3. We will use a technology called AutoLayout to make sure that our new element appears correctly in different screen sizes.

   Make sure that the newly created `UIView` is selected (it will show up highlighted in `UIViewController` within the storyboard and in the navigator sidebar on the left-hand side.)

   Click on the Pin button, highlight the leading, trailing, top, and bottom constraints, disable the **Constrain to margins** option, and make sure that the values of all the constraints are 0.

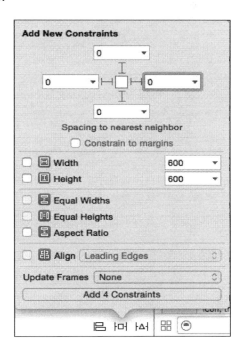

Click on **Add 4 Constraints** to add them. The element will now be centered and will occupy the whole screen, no matter whether it's displayed on an iPad or iPhone in the horizontal or vertical orientation.

4. As the element is still a regular `UIView`, we need to change the class to `MGLMapView`. Click on Identity Inspector and in the **Class** combo box under the **Custom Class** section, type `MGLMapView`. The view will display standard `MGLMapView` instruction text. This means that everything is correct:

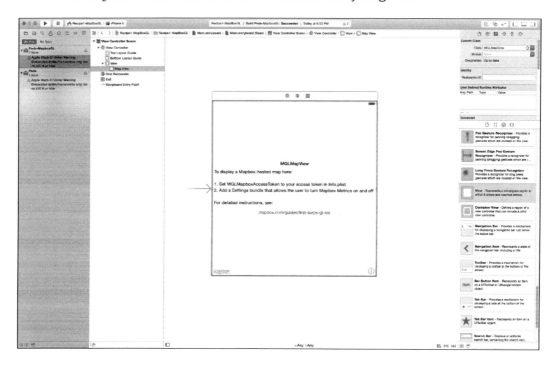

5. We need to be able to reference this element from code. For this, we have to create `IBOutlet`, as follows:

   1. Open Assistant Editor.

   2. Make sure that one side shows the storyboard and the other side shows `ViewController.m`.

   3. Right-click and drag `MGLMapView` in View Controller to the empty area between `@interface ViewController` and `@end`:

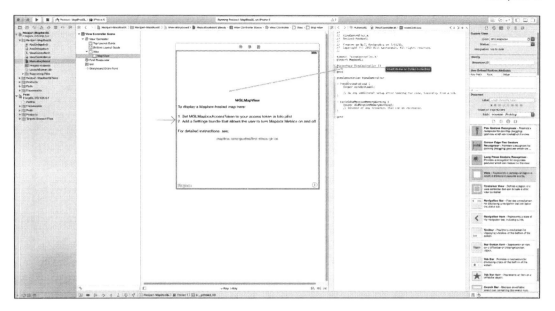

4. Xcode will ask for the name of the outlet. We will name it `mapView` and click on **Connect**. Xcode will automatically create a new `IBOutlet`, as follows:

```
@property (weak, nonatomic) IBOutlet MGLMapView *mapView;
```

6. The next step is to add our Mapbox GL access token to the project. In order to do this, we have to add a new entry to a file called `info.plist`. The easiest way to do this is by opening our target and adding a new entry. Perform the following steps:

   1. Click on your project file in the upper-left corner of Project Navigator.

   2. Click on the target under Targets. Mine is called **Recipe-1-MapBoxGL**, but it depends on how we named the project.

   3. Click on the info option, then select the last entry in **Custom iOS Target Properties** and click on the **+** button.

4. This will add a new entry to the `info.plist` file. Fill the left-hand side (key) with `MGLMapboxAccessToken` and the right-hand side (value) with the actual access token; this will look something similar to the following:

```
pk.eyJ1IjoibWFwYm94cmVjaXBlyIsImEiOiJjd3RhQmlzIn0.
Wx0fWGCo3gs6fzta5QrLfw
```

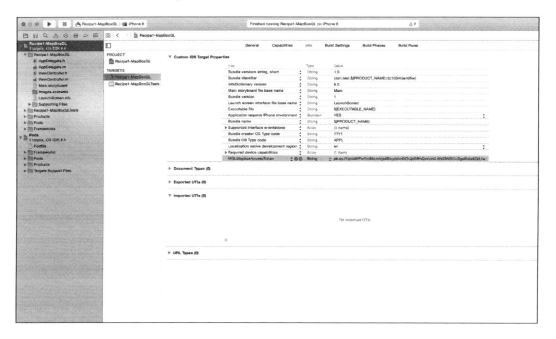

7. Mapbox requires you to add an option for users to opt out of the metrics. This can be done either by creating a settings file or inside the app. In this case, we will add a settings file. Mapbox was kind enough to prepare one for us, so we only need to perform the following steps:

   1. Download the file from `https://github.com/mapbox/mapbox-gl-native/releases/download/ios-v3.1.2/mapbox-ios-sdk-3.1.2.zip`.

   2. Extract the zip folder.

   3. Drag `Settings.bundle` into your project. It's best to drop it over the project file (this is the one with the blue Xcode icon).

   4. A dialog will appear. Make sure that **Copy items if needed** is selected and then click on **Finish**:

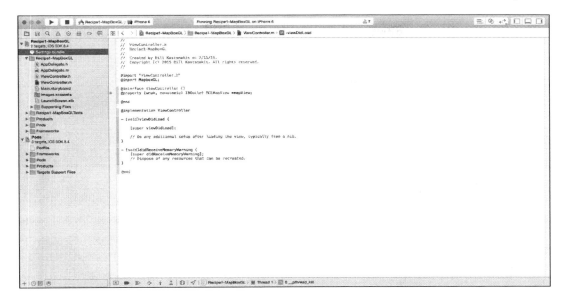

8. Great! Now you can build and run the project to view the results, as in the following screenshot:

Mapbox GL is now correctly linked, and we have built a simple app that displays a Mapbox map! You can use normal gestures, such as panning and pinching, to navigate around this map.

How it works...

The most important component of Mapbox GL is `MGLMapView`. The way it works is exactly how Apple's own MapKit framework works as it uses the same concepts. Be patient; we will explain much more on how it works in the next few recipes. To add it to the project, we will follow the same rules as any `UIView` component. In order for Mapbox GL to work, we need to add our access token to the project's `info.plist` file. The `info.plist` file is a file that exists in every single app. It's often used to set various app settings, such as the version number, and by external frameworks to add their own settings as well.

The last thing needed to integrate Mapbox GL is a settings file. When you open iOS settings, except for the bundled Apple apps, you will often note that it includes third-party apps too. In order to have our app appear in the settings, we need to create this `Settings.bundle` file. We will use it to allow the user to opt out of the metrics, as this is required by Mapbox to comply with privacy.

Switching between locations programmatically

In this recipe, we will learn how to center the map on a specific location programmatically. We will move faster from now on. We will not focus on the iOS SDK anymore, and we will describe the steps related to general iOS development faster than the previous recipes. We will also dedicate our efforts to explaining more about the framework itself.

How to do it...

Follow these steps:

1. Open the `Chapter6-Recipe3-Begin` folder and then the `.xcworkspace` file.

 The project is already set up to be used with CocoaPods, but it doesn't include the dependencies required. Before opening the `.xcworkspace` file in Xcode, don't forget to run the `pod install` command in the root of the project folder to download the dependencies.

We will use this starter project to get through the recipe. In the storyboard, I added `UIToolBar`, two `UIButtonItem` controls, and `UISegmentedControl`. All the controls are linked to `ViewController`. In the `info.plist` file, I also added the `NSLocationWhenInUseUsageDescription` key as it's required to get the user's location.

> You can find more information about the `NSLocationWhenInUseUsageDescription` key in the Apple documentation at https://developer.apple.com/library/ios/documentation/General/Reference/InfoPlistKeyReference/Articles/CocoaKeys.html#//apple_ref/doc/uid/TP40009251-SW27.

2. Jump to the `ViewController.m` file. We will first have to tell Mapbox GL to show the user's location on the map. In `viewDidLoad()`, add the following line:

```
[self.mapView setShowsUserLocation:YES];
```

At the moment when our storyboard's `viewController` file is loaded, the app will request permission from the user to show the user's location. If it's granted, it will show the blue user location dot on the map. If it's not or if it's unable to get the user's location, it will show nothing.

> Geolocation-based apps are always better to test on a real device. If you're testing the app in the iOS simulator, you can get it to simulate the user's location by navigating to **Debug | Location** in the iOS simulator menu. You can select from a list of predefined locations or use **Custom** and type your own coordinates.

3. Now, we will create the functionality to switch between San Francisco and the user's location. In the `(IBAction)centerToLocation:(id)sender` method, add the following code:

```
- (IBAction)centerToLocation:(id)sender {

    if ([self.button.title isEqualToString:kButtonCenterTitle]) {

        [self.button setTitle:kButtonUserTitle];

        CLLocationCoordinate2D sanFrancisco =
CLLocationCoordinate2DMake(37.775934, -122.432499);
```

```
        [self.mapView setCenterCoordinate:sanFrancisco
zoomLevel:12 animated:YES];


    } else {

        [self.button setTitle:kButtonCenterTitle];

        CLLocationCoordinate2D userLocation = [self.mapView.
userLocation coordinate];
        [self.mapView setCenterCoordinate:userLocation zoomLevel:7
animated:YES];


    }
}
```

In the preceding code, if the button title is `Center`, we will create a new coordinate using the `CLLocationCoordinate2D` struct.

The struct accepts latitude and longitude, and each one is `CLLocationDegrees`, as follows:

```
typedef struct { CLLocationDegrees latitude; CLLocationDegrees
longitude; }
```

`CLLocationDegrees` is actually nothing more than a double type value. After we have created our coordinate variable, we will use the following function:

```
setCenterCoordinate:zoomLevel:animated
```

This function will center the map at the coordinates passed and at a specific zoom level, and we can choose whether we want it to animate the change from the old location to the new one.

If you used Apple's own MapKit framework, you're probably already starting to understand the benefits and the ease of use of Mapbox GL. In MapKit, you passed `MKCoordinateSpan` to specify the zoom level, which represents the amount of distance from north to south and east to west. In order to do something simple, such as zooming to a specific zoom level—a familiar terminology for geolocation apps—we had to do the math, and it was generally much harder than simply passing an integer. After the `else` part, we repeated the process, but instead of passing coordinates, we got the coordinates of the user's location from `mapView`, as follows:

```
CLLocationCoordinate2D userLocation = [self.mapView.userLocation
coordinate];
```

4. This is all we need to zoom to a specific location programmatically. Build and run the project on a device or in a simulator (don't forget to simulate the location) and click on the **Center** button in UIToolBar.

How it works...

Let's explain in a little more detail what we can do with MGLMapView. We can use centerCoordinate to get or set the center of mapView. It can also animate the transition from the old center to the new one. We can use zoomLevel to set or get the zoom level programmatically. Using visibleCoordinateBounds, we can get or set the bounds of the map. We can also change the heading of the map using the setDirection:animated method.

Adding markers to the map

A map without points of interest is less useful. In this recipe, you will learn how to generate **markers,** or **annotations** as they are called in iOS terminology.

How to do it...

Follow these steps:

1. Open the `Chapter6-Recipe4-Begin` folder and then the `.xcworkspace` file in Xcode. This project contains the project as it ended in the previous recipe.

2. The **+** button is already connected in the storyboard to our `viewController.m` file's following method:

   ```
   - (IBAction)addAnnotation:(id)sender
   ```

   We first need to initialize a new annotation. We will first create a new `MGLPointAnnoation` object. Within the `- (IBAction)addAnnotation:(id) sender` context, add the following line:

   ```
   MGLPointAnnotation *annotation = [[MGLPointAnnotation alloc]
   init];
   ```

3. The next step is to pass the coordinates; run the following command for this:

   ```
   [annotation setCoordinate:self.mapView.centerCoordinate];
   ```

   Here, `self.mapView.centerCoordinate` will create the annotation at the center of our map. It will always be at the center, even if we pan around the map before creating the annotation.

4. Optionally, we can pass a title and subtitle as follows:

   ```
   [annotation setTitle:@"Here!"];
   [annotation setSubtitle:@"We have created an annotation"];
   ```

   When you tap on the annotation, a callout will pop up with the title and subtitle.

5. The last step is to add the annotation to the map. We will do this via the following:

```
[self.mapView addAnnotation:annotation];
```

6. As we have a title and a subtitle, we have to instruct Mapbox GL that we want to show callouts. For this, we need to conform to a specific `MGLMapViewDelegate` protocol method. Therefore, execute the following command:

```
- (BOOL)mapView:(MGLMapView *)mapView annotationCanShowCallout:(id
<MGLAnnotation>)annotation {

    return YES;

}
```

Returning `YES` from `mapView:annoationCanShowCallout:annotation` will show the callout for every annotation we create. The reason Mapbox GL uses a delegate method for this is that we can easily use logic to show the callout on selected annotations.

7. The last step is to make sure that our `ViewController` conforms to `MGLMapViewDelegate`.

There are two ways to do this. The first is as follows:

1. Open the storyboard and in Document Outline, right-click on the `MapView` object and drag a connection to the `ViewController` object.

2. Select **Delegate**, and the connection will be created.

The second way is as follows:

1. Add the following line in `viewDidLoad`:

```
[self.mapView setDelegate:self];
```

2. Make sure that `viewController` conforms to `MGLMapViewDelegate`. You can add `<MGLMapViewDelegate>` in `ViewController.h` at the `@interface` part or in the `.m` file:

```
@interface ViewController () <MGLMapViewDelegate>
```

8. Build and run the project. Try to pan and zoom around the map. Click on the **+** button to create new annotations, as shown in the following screenshot:

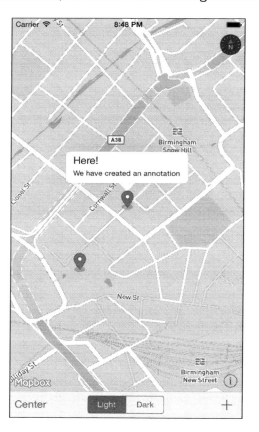

How it works...

We can add new annotations to the map using `addAnnotation:` or multiple markers using `addAnnotations:`. The annotations added to the map will be stored to the `MGLMapView` annotations array, which is a read-only property. We can use this if we want to get an annotation that already exists on the map or check whether an annotation has already been added. To remove annotations from the map, we can use `removeAnnotation:` and `removeAnnotations:`, respectively.

`MGLMapView` conforms to the `MGLMapViewDelegate` protocol. Using this optional set of methods, we can further customize how annotations react.

For example, we will use `(BOOL)mapView:(MGLMapView *)mapView annotationCanS howCallout:(id<MGLAnnotation>)annotation` to return if we want each annotation to show a callout. The benefit of this is that we can add more logic in this method, for example, if we want some annotations to show a callout as opposed to others.

Another delegate method we used in this recipe is the following:

```
- (nullable MGLAnnotationImage *)mapView:(MGLMapView *)mapView imageFo
rAnnotation:(id<MGLAnnotation>)annotation
```

The purpose again is that further logic can be added to have different images for different annotations. This specific method uses a mechanism called **dequeuing**. What this does is to recycle the annotation images to save resources. Once `MGLAnnotationImage` goes offscreen, it can be dequeued and reused. You will learn more `MGLMapViewDelegate` methods in the next few recipes.

There's more...

How about custom icons on the markers? The only thing needed is to conform to another delegate method named `mapView:imageForAnnotation`.

Let's do this right now, as follows:

1. Open the `ViewController.m` file in Xcode.
2. Add the following code:

```
- (MGLAnnotationImage *)mapView:(MGLMapView *)mapView
imageForAnnotation:(id <MGLAnnotation>)annotation {

  MGLAnnotationImage *annotationImage = [mapView dequeueReusableAn
notationImageWithIdentifier:kMapShooping];

  if (!annotationImage) {

    annotationImage = [MGLAnnotationImage annotationImageWithImage
:[UIImage imageNamed:@"Repair"] reuseIdentifier:kMapRepair];

  }

  return annotationImage;
}
```

Let's explain what happens in this code. We first need to dequeue a new annotation. Dequeuing is a common term used in iOS development; for example, it is heavily used in `UITableViews` and `UICollectionViews`.

What it does is to help optimize the map in terms of memory usage and speed by reusing the markers. When we pan or zoom the map and a marker goes offscreen, it becomes available for reuse. In the first line, we asked `mapView` to dequeue a new `MGLAnnotationImage`, as follows:

```
MGLAnnotationImage *annotationImage = [mapView dequeueReusableAnnota
tionImageWithIdentifier:kMapShooping];
```

A map can use multiple kinds of markers, which are grouped by identifiers such as `UITableViewCells`. In this case, we used a single type of marker and a single identifier. The next step is to check whether the map returned `MGLAnnotationImage`. It will come back empty in the following cases:

▶   If this is the first object we created

▶   If we didn't scroll or zoom due to which an object is outside the visible screen

In the next few lines, we can take care of this case:

```
if (!annotationImage) {

    annotationImage = [MGLAnnotationImage
        annotationImageWithImage:[UIImage imageNamed:@"Repair"]
        reuseIdentifier:kMapRepair];

}
```

So, if nothing comes back from the dequeuing process, we will create a new `MGLAnnotationImage` with the image we want.

 The icon images used in this project are contained in a file called **asset catalog** (`.xcassets`). In this case, they are inside the `MapIcons.xcassets` file.

This is all we need to create a custom marker. Now, build and run the project:

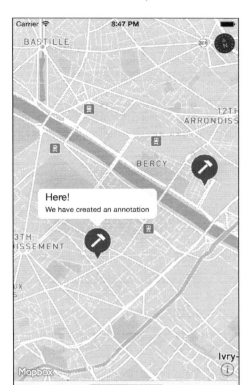

Switching map styles

In this recipe, you will learn how to switch between different map styles. The project contains `UISegmentedControl` with two states: light and dark. It's connected to the `switchMapStyle:sender` IBAction of `ViewController`. We will implement the functionality needed to switch between the light and dark styles.

How to do it...

Follow these steps:

1. We will continue with the project as we left it in the previous recipe. Jump over to the `ViewController.m` file.

2. Replace the `switchMapStyle:sender` method with the following code:

```
- (IBAction)switchMapStyle:(id)sender {

    if ([sender isKindOfClass:[UISegmentedControl class]]) {

        UISegmentedControl *segmentedControl = (UISegmentedControl
*)sender;

        if (segmentedControl.selectedSegmentIndex == 0) {

            NSURL *lightStyle = [NSURL URLWithString:@"asset://
styles/light-v7.json"];
            [self.mapView setStyleURL:lightStyle];

        } else {

            NSURL *darkStyle = [NSURL URLWithString:@"asset://
styles/dark-v7.json"];
            [self.mapView setStyleURL:darkStyle];

        }

    }

}
```

Let's explain how this method works. Mapbox GL contains several predefined map styles, which are as follows:

- `dark-v7.json`: This a dark style map and is great for overlays with bright markers or polygons
- `mapbox-streets-v7.json`: This is the standard Mapbox Streets style optimized for mobile devices
- `emerald-v7.json`: This is a great style for terrain and transportation
- `satellite-v7.json`: This is used for satellite imagery
- `light-v7.json`: This is a light-themed style, which is great with dark markers or polygons

In the preceding code, we first checked whether the sender was our UISegmentedControl, then we switched the style based on the button selection by getting the NSURL of the style we wanted and passing it to mapView using setStyleURL, as follows:

```
        NSURL *lightStyle = [NSURL URLWithString:@"asset://
styles/light-v7.json"];
        [self.mapView setStyleURL:lightStyle];
```

3. Build and run the project. Try to switch the segmented control to switch the style.

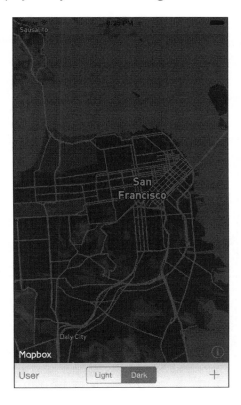

4. You may notice that the project starts with the default map style, which is mapbox-streets-v7.json, while UISegmentedControl has the light-v7.json style as the default.

In order for the project to open with the light style preselected, you can optionally repeat the following lines of code in viewDidLoad:

```
        NSURL *lightStyle = [NSURL URLWithString:@"asset://
styles/light-v7.json"];
        [self.mapView setStyleURL:lightStyle];
```

There's more...

We have already discussed how we can select one of the predefined styles that comes with Mapbox GL. Now, we will focus on how we can load raster tiles. We generated raster tiles using TileMill in the previous chapters. Here are the steps:

1. We will continue from the point where we left off in the previous recipe. First, we need to create a new file. In Xcode, go to the **File** menu and navigate to **New | File**.

2. The file dialog will open. Select the **Other** category and the **Empty** file.

3. Name the file `rasterstyle.json` and click on **Create**.

4. A new file will be created. Now, select this file and write the following JSON:

```
{
    "version": 7,
    "sources": {
       "tiles": {
            "type": "raster",
            "url": "mapbox://mapboxrecipes.utftest",
            "tileSize": 256
        }
    },
    "layers": [
            {
            "id": "tiles",
            "type": "raster",
            "source": "tiles"
            }
            ]
}
```

This file will instruct Mapbox GL on where to fetch the tiles. If the tiles are hosted on the Mapbox server, this is how it is supposed to be. The most important value here is that of `url`. Replace this value with your own Map ID.

If the tiles are hosted on another server, you must create a JSON code, as shown here:

```
{
    "version": 7,
    "name": "Raster Tiles",
    "sources": {
      "yourTileLayer": {
        "type": "raster",
        "tiles": [
          "https://1.tile.server/{z}/{x}/{y}.png",
          "https://2.tile.server/{z}/{x}/{y}.png"
        ],
        "tileSize": 256
      }
    },
    "layers": [{
      "id": "yourTileLayer",
      "type": "raster",
      "source": "yourTileLayer",
      "paint": {
        "raster-fade-duration": 100
      }
    }]
}
```

5. Save the file.

6. Head over to the `ViewController.m` file. In `viewDidLoad:`, copy the following code:

```
NSURL *styleURL = [NSURL URLWithString:@"asset://../../../
rasterstyle.json"];
    [self.mapView setStyleURL:styleURL];

    CLLocationCoordinate2D coordinate =
CLLocationCoordinate2DMake(39.452101, -100.986328);
    [self.mapView setCenterCoordinate:coordinate zoomLevel:5
animated:NO];
```

As in the previous recipe, we will use `setStyleURL` to set the map style. The `//../../../` may need to be adjusted based on your project structure.

As raster tiles are usually generated for a specific area and zoom level, we will center the map at a location where the tiles are visible.

7. Build and run the project.

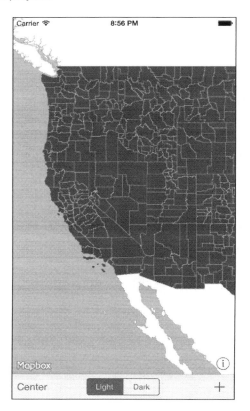

One more thing...

You learned how we can use the predefined map styles in Mapbox GL. While the predefined styles may serve our purpose, there are cases where we need to customize the map style, as we did in the previous chapters using CartoCSS with Mapbox Studio and TileMill.

Well, there is good news and bad news. The good news is that we can create our own custom styles. The bad news is that the styling language, while it looks similar to CartoCSS, isn't the same, and there is no editor similar to Mapbox Studio that can help us create our styles. At the moment of writing this chapter, which is August 2015, Mapbox has already announced that they are working on an editor, but it's not released yet.

In this recipe, you will learn how we can create our own custom styles:

1. We will use the same project as in the previous recipe. Open it in Xcode, and inside our application bundle, create a new empty JSON file as we did in the previous recipe. Name the file `customstyle.json`.

2. Copy the following code into `customstyle.json`:

```json
{
    "version": 1,
    "name": "customstyle.json",
    "constants": {
        "@water": "#66bbdd",
        "@land": "#ffffff"
    },
    "sources": {
        "mapbox-streets": {
            "type": "vector",
            "url": "mapbox://mapbox.mapbox-streets-v6"
        }
    },
    "layers": [{
                "id": "background",
                "type": "background",
                "layout": {
                "visibility": "visible"
                },
                "paint": {
                "background-color": "@land"
                }
                },
                {
                "id": "water",
                "source": "mapbox-streets",
                "source-layer": "water",
                "type": "fill",
                "paint":{
                "fill-color": "@water"
                }
                }
                ],
        "owner": "billkastanakis","id": "mapboxrecipes.000000"
}
```

To create the style of the map, we will use **Mapbox GL Style Reference**. It tells the renderer from which sources to fetch the data, what to draw and in which order, and how to style our layers.

 The Mapbox GL Style Reference documentation can be found at
https://www.mapbox.com/mapbox-gl-style-spec/#symbol.

At the version and name keys, you can give any version and name to your custom map. The constants key is used to create color constants to make our lives easier, just as we did in CartoCSS. At the sources key, we will define which sources we will use in this custom style. Sources can be mapbox.mapbox-terrain-v2, mapbox://mapbox.mapbox-streets-v6, mapbox://mapbox.satellite, or a combination of these. Version numbers also vary. At the layers key, we will define which layers we will use in this custom style. We will use id to get the layer ID from a specific source. Then, we can modify this layer's attributes the same way as we did in CartoCSS.

3. Make sure you have saved your customstyle.json file.

4. In ViewController.m, we can load the custom style in the exact same way as we defined the predefined and raster styles. Modify viewDidLoad: to do exactly this, as follows:

```
    NSURL *styleURL = [NSURL URLWithString:@"asset://../../../
customstyle.json"];
    [self.mapView setStyleURL:styleURL];

    CLLocationCoordinate2D coordinate =
CLLocationCoordinate2DMake(39.452101, -100.986328);
    [self.mapView setCenterCoordinate:coordinate zoomLevel:2
animated:NO];
```

5. Build and run the project. Our custom style will be loaded as shown in the following screenshot:

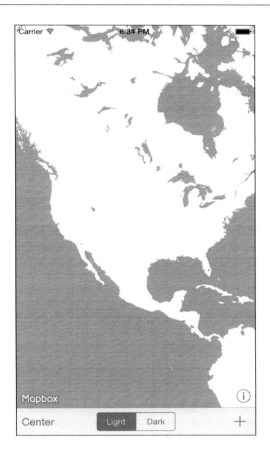

How it works...

In Mapbox GL, we can use predefined styles; there are four at the time of writing this chapter.

To use them, we will simply call `setStyleURL:` and pass `NSURL` of the style we want. Additionally, we can fetch raster tiles. To do this, we need to create a new JSON object that informs Mapbox GL where to find the tiles we want. We will then use the same `setStyleURL` method to set the style to our custom JSON object.

The last option is to create our own custom style. To do this, we need to use Mapbox GL Style, which is an object describing to Mapbox GL what to draw and in which order and how to style the map. Due to the lack of tools at the time of writing, we again have to create a JSON object, specify the sources we want to fetch the data from, and then customize the layers displayed.

Loading GeoJSON and drawing a polyline

In this recipe, you will learn how to parse a GeoJSON file and draw a polyline on the map using Mapbox GL. This will be a great start if your purpose is to create applications that draw routes on a map.

How to do it...

Perform the following steps:

1. Open the `Chapter6-Recipe6-Begin` folder and then the `.xcworkspace` file. This project contains a basic Mapbox GL map. It uses the **emerald** style, which is the best-looking style to display directions. The project also contains a `route.geojson` file. Normally, you would fetch the data from a service, but for the purpose of this recipe, we will use a file stored in our bundle.

2. Our first step is to parse the GeoJSON file and get the coordinates contained in the `geometry.coordinates` array under the features. We will do this in a separate method, as follows:

```
- (void)loadGeoJSONFile {

    dispatch_queue_t queue = dispatch_get_global_queue
        (DISPATCH_QUEUE_PRIORITY_DEFAULT, 0);

    dispatch_async(queue, ^{

        NSString *path = [[NSBundle mainBundle]
pathForResource:@"route" ofType:@"geojson"];

        NSData *geoJSONData = [NSData
dataWithContentsOfFile:path];

        NSDictionary *geoJSON = [NSJSONSerialization
JSONObjectWithData:geoJSONData options:0 error:nil];

for (NSDictionary *feature in [geoJSON valueForKey:@"features"]) {
        NSArray *coordinates = [feature
valueForKeyPath:@"geometry.coordinates"];
            [self drawPolylineWithCoordinates:coordinates];
        }

    });

}
```

Let's dissect this method. We will use **Grand Central Dispatch** (**GCD**) to parse the array into a background thread. We do not want to freeze the UI while parsing the GeoJSON file, especially if the file is big.

Within the `dispatch_async` block, we will get the path to the GeoJSON file stored in the app bundle via the following command:

```
NSString *path = [[NSBundle mainBundle]
pathForResource:@"route" ofType:@"geojson"];
```

Next, we will load the data, as follows:

```
NSData *geoJSONData = [NSData
dataWithContentsOfFile:path];
```

`NSData dataWithContentsOfFile` is a synchronous call. This means that the UI will freeze while in progress. This is why we used the background thread.

Next, we will convert the data into `NSDictionary`. The `NSJSONSerialization` will do the job for us, as follows:

```
NSDictionary *geoJSON = [NSJSONSerialization
JSONObjectWithData:geoJSONData options:0 error:nil];
```

Now, we will enumerate through the features and create a new `NSArray` with the coordinates under the `geometry.coordinates` key in the JSON file, as follows:

```
for (NSDictionary *feature in [geoJSON
valueForKey:@"features"]) {
        NSArray *coordinates = [feature
valueForKeyPath:@"geometry.coordinates"];
        [self drawPolylineWithCoordinates:coordinates];
    }
```

Finally, we will call `[self drawPolylineWithCoordinates:coordinates]` and pass the `NSArray` coordinates we just created.

The `drawPolylineWithCoordinates` method isn't created yet, so let's do this now.

3. Let's create the `drawPolylineWithCoordinates` method. In this method, we will pass the `NSArray` coordinates created previously, as follows:

```
dispatch_async(dispatch_get_main_queue(), ^{

    int coordinatesCount = (int)[coordinatesArray count];
    CLLocationCoordinate2D coordinates[coordinatesCount];

    for (int i=0; i<coordinatesArray.count; i++) {
```

```
         NSArray *point = [coordinatesArray objectAtIndex:i];
         CLLocationCoordinate2D coordinate = CLLocationCoordina
te2DMake([point[1] doubleValue], [point[0] doubleValue]);
         coordinates[i] = coordinate;

    }

    MGLPolyline *polyline = [MGLPolyline polylineWithCoordinat
es:coordinates count:[coordinatesArray count]];
    [self.mapView addAnnotation:polyline];
    [self.mapView setVisibleCoordinates:coordinates
count:coordinatesCount edgePadding:UIEdgeInsetsMake(50, 50, 50,
50) animated:YES];

    });
```

First, we will use GCD again to execute the code in the main thread. For this, we will use `dispatch_async(dispatch_get_main_queue()` and include the rest of the code within the block.

Next, we will create an empty `CLLocationCoordinates2D` array. `CLLocationCoordinates2D` is just a C struct that contains latitude and longitude, as in the following lines:

```
    int coordinatesCount = (int)[coordinatesArray count];
    CLLocationCoordinate2D coordinates[coordinatesCount];
```

> `CLLocationCoordinate2D` is actually a struct used by Apple's own MapKit framework. One of the strengths of Mapbox GL is that it uses the same concepts as Apple's native frameworks to make our lives easier, as follows:
>
> ```
> typedef struct {
>    CLLocationDegrees latitude;
>    CLLocationDegrees longitude;
> } CLLocationCoordinate2D;
> ```

The next step is to loop through each point in `coordinatesArray`, which we passed earlier, and fill the newly created `coordinates[]` with `CLLocationCoordinates2D`:

1. We will get each point from `NSArray`; execute the following command:

    ```
    NSArray *point = [coordinatesArray objectAtIndex:i];
    ```

2. We will generate a new `CLLocationCoordinate2D` array, where we will pass the second element as the latitude and the first as the longitude, as our GeoJSON file contains these values in this order. Run the following:

```
CLLocationCoordinate2D coordinate = CLLocationCoordinate2DMa
ke([point[1] doubleValue], [point[0] doubleValue]);
```

3. Finally, we will add the `CLLocationCoordinate2D` array in the `coordinates[]` array via the following line:

```
coordinates[i] = coordinate;
```

Then, we will create a new `MGLPolyline` and pass the coordinates, which is just an open line consisting of one or more points. The points are connected in the order that they are provided. `MGLPolyline` needs the array of `CLLocationCoordinates2D` as the first parameter and the count of the elements contained in the array as the second parameter, as follows:

```
MGLPolyline *polyline = [MGLPolyline polylineWithCoordinates:coord
inates count:[coordinatesArray count]];
```

On the next line, we will add the polyline to the map, as follows:

```
[self.mapView addAnnotation:polyline];
```

Finally, we will center and zoom the map to fit our polyline, as in the following lines:

```
[self.mapView setVisibleCoordinates:coordinates
count:coordinatesCount edgePadding:UIEdgeInsetsMake(50, 50, 50,
50) animated:YES];
```

The `setVisibleCoordinates` accepts an array of `coordinates[]` containing `CLLocationCoordinate2D` elements as the first value. The `count` is the number of elements contained in the array. The `edgePadding` is another C struct that represents the top, left, bottom, and right edges in this order. The values are in screen points; so, in this case, we will set a padding of 50 points on each side.

4. Finally, we will call `[self loadGeoJSONFile]` in the `viewDidAppear` method just to make sure that the map is loaded and drawn on screen before we attempt to add the polyline. Execute the following:

```
- (void)viewDidAppear:(BOOL)animated {

    [super viewDidAppear:animated];
    [self loadGeoJSONFile];

}
```

5. Next, in order to customize the color and line width of `MGLPolyline`, we need to conform to the following `MGLMapViewDelegate` methods:

```
- (CGFloat)mapView:(MGLMapView *)mapView lineWidthForPolylineAnnot
ation:(MGLPolyline *)annotation {
    return 5.0f;
}

- (UIColor *)mapView:(MGLMapView *)mapView strokeColorForShapeAnno
tation:(MGLShape *)annotation {
    return [UIColor blueColor];
}
```

In the first method, which is `mapView:lineWidthForPolylineAnnotation`, we returned a float to set the line width to 5.0. In the second method, which is `mapView :strokeColorForShapeAnnotation`, we returned a `UIColor` value of blue.

6. This is all. Now build and run the project:

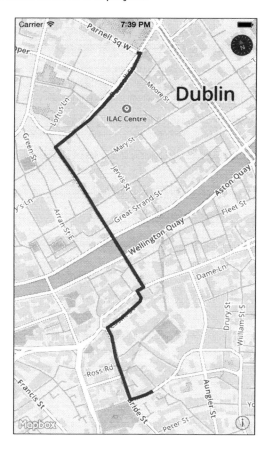

How it works...

To create polylines, we need to create a new `MGLPolyline` object and pass an array of `CLLocationCoordinates2D` structs. Each struct in the array represents a point and contains the latitude and longitude. To add the polyline to the map, we used the `addAnnotation:` method. As you probably noticed, whatever we add to the map is called an annotation, no matter whether it's a marker, polyline, or polygon. We can then access the polyline using the `annotations` array in the `MGLMapView` object. As the array is read-only, we can't modify it directly, and to remove the polyline, we have to go through `removeAnnotation:` if required. To customize the polyline appearance, we used the `MGLMapViewDelegate` methods `mapView:lineWidthForPolylineAnnotation:` and `mapView:strokeColorForShapeAnnotation:`. In the first one, we simply returned a float as the width of the polyline, and in the second one, we used `UIColor` to set the color.

Drawing polygons on the map

In this recipe, you will learn how to draw polygons on the map. We will create an app that allows the user to click on the map to add a point to a preexisting polygon.

How to do it...

Perform the following steps:

1. Open the `Chapter6-Recipe7-Begin` folder and then the `.xcworkspace` file. The project contains the usual Mapbox GL map already set up in the storyboard. Additionally, I added `UITapGestureRecognizer` and connected it to the following:

   - `(IBAction)tapgestureRecognizerTapped:(id)sender`

   When the gesture recognizer is tapped, it will trigger the action.

2. First, we need to create a basic polygon and add it to the map. We will do this in a new function, as follows:

   ```
   - (void)drawInitialPolygon {

       CLLocationCoordinate2D coordinates[] = {
           CLLocationCoordinate2DMake(53.359016, -6.261907),
           CLLocationCoordinate2DMake(53.355994, -6.265082),
           CLLocationCoordinate2DMake(53.352510, -6.261392)
       };

       NSUInteger count = sizeof(coordinates) /
   sizeof(CLLocationCoordinate2D);
   ```

```
    MGLPolygon *polygon = [MGLPolygon polygonWithCoordinates:coord
inates count:count];

    [self.mapView addAnnotation:polygon];

}
```

Let's dissect this function:

- ❏ We first created a new `coordinates[]` array containing `CLLocationCoordinates` structs, as we did in the previous recipe, via the following lines:

  ```
  CLLocationCoordinate2D coordinates[] = {
    CLLocationCoordinate2DMake(53.359016, -6.261907),
      CLLocationCoordinate2DMake(53.355994, -6.265082),
        CLLocationCoordinate2DMake(53.352510, -6.261392)
    };
  ```

- ❏ We counted the number of elements in `coordinatesArray[]`, as follows:

  ```
  NSUInteger count = sizeof(coordinates) /
  sizeof(CLLocationCoordinate2D);
  ```

- ❏ Then, we generated a new `MGLPolygon`:

  ```
  MGLPolygon *polygon = [MGLPolygon polygonWithCoordinates:coo
  rdinates count:count];
  ```

  The `MGLPolygon` class represents a closed shape that consists of one or more points. The points are connected in the order provided, similar to `MGLPolyline` in the previous recipe. It accepts an array of `CLLocationCordinate2D` structs as the first parameter and the count of the array as the second parameter.

- ❏ Finally, we added the `MGLPolygon` class to the map via the following:

  ```
  [self.mapView addAnnotation:polygon];
  ```

3. We need to call our new method to `viewDidAppear` to make sure that the map is on screen before attempting to draw the polygon. We can do this by executing the following:

```
- (void)viewDidAppear:(BOOL)animated {
    [super viewDidAppear:animated];
    [self drawInitialPolygon];
}
```

4. To customize the fill and stroke of the polygon, we need to conform to the following `MGKMapViewDelegate` protocol methods:

```
- (CGFloat)mapView:(MGLMapView *)mapView lineWidthForPolylineAnnot
ation:(MGLPolyline *)annotation {
    return 5.0f;
}

- (UIColor *)mapView:(MGLMapView *)mapView strokeColorForShapeAnno
tation:(MGLShape *)annotation {
    return [UIColor blueColor];
}

- (UIColor *)mapView:(MGLMapView *)mapView fillColorForPolygonAnno
tation:(MGLPolygon *)annotation {
    return [UIColor colorWithRed:154.0f/255.0f green:58.0f/255.0f
blue:18.0f/255.0f alpha:0.5f];
}
```

We have already seen the first two methods. In the third one, `mapView:fillCol orForPolygonAnnotation:`, we need to return `UIColor` as the fill color of the annotation. We will return a semitransparent orange color.

5. At this point, you can build and run the recipe if you wish. The polygon will appear on the screen as it does in the following screenshot:

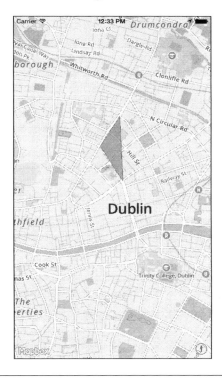

6. Let's continue with the recipe. We need to add a new point to the already created polygon when the user taps on the screen. We will do this inside the - (IBAction) tapgestureRecognizerTapped: (id)sender method, so let's overwrite it with the following code:

```
- (IBAction)tapgestureRecognizerTapped:(id)sender {

    // Get the tapped point from the view
    CGPoint point = [self.tapGestureRecognizer
locationInView:self.view];

    // Convert it into map coordinates
    CLLocationCoordinate2D tappedCoordinate = [self.mapView
convertPoint:point toCoordinateFromView:self.view];

    // Get the polygon from the map
    MGLPolygon *polygon = [self.mapView.annotations firstObject];

    // Create a new empty coordinates array with +1 elements
    NSUInteger count = [polygon pointCount];
    CLLocationCoordinate2D coordinates[count + 1];

    // Get the points from the polygons
    [polygon getCoordinates:coordinates range:NSMakeRange(0,
count)];

    // Add the new coordinate we just tapped.
    coordinates[count] = tappedCoordinate;

    // Remove the old polygon from the map.
    [self.mapView removeAnnotation:polygon];

    // Create a new polygon and add it again.
    MGLPolygon *newPolygon = [MGLPolygon polygonWithCoordinates:co
ordinates count:count + 1];
    [self.mapView addAnnotation:newPolygon];

}
```

Let's dissect the preceding code:

- ❑ First, we need to get the point that the user tapped; the following lines will help us do this:

  ```
  CGPoint point = [self.tapGestureRecognizer
  locationInView:self.view];
  ```

- ❑ The point is in screen coordinates, so we need to convert it into CLLocationCoordinate2D, which uses the **WGS84** standard, as follows:

  ```
  CLLocationCoordinate2D tappedCoordinate = [self.mapView
  convertPoint:point toCoordinateFromView:self.view];
  ```

- ❑ We already have a polygon on the map. Let's grab it via the following:

  ```
  MGLPolygon *polygon = [self.mapView.annotations
  firstObject];
  ```

  Our mapView object contains an array of the annotations we added. These could be markers, polylines, polygons, or a mix of all three. Normally, we should add some logic here to get the object we want, but in this case, we only have a simple polygon.

- ❑ Now, we need to create a new polygon; however, first, we will need a new array to hold the coordinates. So, run the following:

  ```
  NSUInteger count = [polygon pointCount];
  CLLocationCoordinate2D coordinates[count + 1];
  ```

  We had three elements before, so the new array will have the previous three points plus the newly tapped coordinate for a total of four.

- ❑ Let's grab the points from the polygon that is on screen via the following:

  ```
  [polygon getCoordinates:coordinates range:NSMakeRange(0,
  count)];
  ```

  MGLPolygon inherits from GKLMultipoint, which has the getCoordinates:range method. It will return the points as a **C array** passed as the first parameter. The C array must have enough elements to hold the number of coordinates returned by the function. In the range parameter, you can specify how many points you want back, but in this case, we will tell it to return all the elements.

- ❏ At this point, we have the three elements stored in the `coordinates` array, but we still need to add the newly created coordinate that was generated when the user tapped on the screen. So we will execute the following:

  ```
  coordinates[count] = tappedCoordinate;
  ```

- ❏ Remove the polygon that is currently on screen through the following line:

  ```
  [self.mapView removeAnnotation:polygon];
  ```

- ❏ Finally, generate a new polygon and add it to the `mapView` object, as follows:

  ```
  MGLPolygon *newPolygon = [MGLPolygon polygonWithCoordinates:
  coordinates count:count + 1];
  [self.mapView addAnnotation:newPolygon];
  ```

7. Build and run the project and try tapping on the screen at various locations of the map:

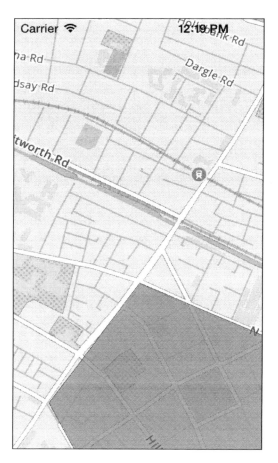

How it works...

MGLPolygon works in exactly the same way as MGLPolyline. It accepts an array of CLLocationCoordinate2D structs as points to draw the closed polygon. We used UIGestureRecognizer, which is defined in the storyboard. The gesture recognizer will trigger the action we specified each time the user taps on the map. Once the user taps, we will have the touch location in the screen's coordinate space. To convert it into latitude and longitude, we will use convertPoint:toCoordinateFromView: of Mapbox GL and pass the touch point and the view we want to convert from, respectively. If we want to do the opposite, we can use convertCoordinate:toPointToView: to convert a map coordinate into CGPoint.

Once we have the coordinates, we will get the MGLPolygon from the annotations array of MGLMapView, and add the new latitude and longitude; then, we will remove the old MGLPolygon from the map and add a new one that also contains the touch location.

Index